a second zen reader

First published by Routledge & Kegan Paul Ltd., London, 1964
Second edition published by Charles E. Tuttle Publishing Co., 1988
Third edition published by The Buddhist Society Trust, 2018
© The Trevor Leggett Adhyatma Yoga Trust, 2018

The publisher gratefully acknowledges the generous contribution
to this book provided by The Trevor Leggett Adhyatma Yoga Trust.

ISBN: 978-0-901032-51-5 (The Buddhist Society Trust)

A catalogue record for this book is available from the British Library

Note on illustrations: The illustrations in this book were first
published in Hannya Shingyo Kowa by Obora Ryoun, published
by Daihorin in 1938.

Edited by Sarah Auld
Designed by Avni Patel

Printed in Padstow, Cornwall by TJ International

a second zen reader

The Tiger's Cave and Translations
of Other Zen Writings

Trevor Leggett

われをのせて
舟のほか
われをも

"If you want a tiger's cub,
you must go into the tiger's cave."
– Zen Saying

To the late Dr. Hari Prasad Shastri, who knew and loved Japan and her people, these translations from the Japanese are reverently dedicated.

Contents

8   Introduction

12   PART ONE

ON THE HEART SUTRA BY ABBOT OBORA

OF THE SOTO ZEN SECT (CONTEMPORARY)

1 The Immutable Scripture

2 The Circle of Life

3 Awakening to the Character of our Individuality

4 The True Character of the Human Self

5 Transcendence

6 The Experience of Emptiness

7 The Bodhisattva Spirit

8 The Experience of Nirvana

9 The Power of Prajna

134   PART TWO

YASENKANNA AN AUTOBIOGRAPHICAL NARRATIVE

BY ZEN MASTER HAKUIN (EIGHTEENTH CENTURY)

1 Introductory Note by The Translator

2 The Preface by a disciple, Cold Starveling,
Master of Poverty Temple

3 Yasenkanna by Hakuin

166 **PART THREE**

THE TIGER'S CAVE AND OTHER PIECES

1 The Tiger's Cave
2 The Lotus in the Mire
3 Poems by Zen master Mamiya
4 The Dance of the Sennin
5 Maxims of Saigo

184 **PART FOUR**

ZEN BY ROSEN TAKASHINA,

PRIMATE OF THE SOTO ZEN SECT

1 The Sermon of No Words
2 Stillness in Action

190 **PART FIVE**

FROM A COMMENTARY ON RINZAI-ROKU

205 List of Illustrations

Introduction

ZEN IS A JAPANESE approximation to the Sanskrit *dhyana*, which has in Yoga the technical meaning of *stilling* and *focussing* the mind. When after long practice all associations have dropped away and the mind is identified with the subtle constituents of the object, the state is called Samadhi of a particular kind. In that Samadhi there finally comes a flash of intuitive knowledge or Prajna, which reveals the truth of the object of meditation. Prajna is knowledge not coming by the routes of sense-perception, inference or authority: it is immediate and invariably correct.

Buddhism adopted Yoga methods, and dhyana discipline was the final step before realisation. The Zen sect, founded in China by the Indian patriarch Bodhidharma, lays special emphasis on meditation practice, and claims a special tradition handed down 'from heart to heart' from the Buddha himself. The main tenets of Buddhism and of Zen will be found in Abbot Obora's Heart Sutra commentary in this book, and they need not be summarised here.

In Zen as in other mystical schools there are spiritual crises, and the teacher has a very important role in resolving them. The teacher does not normally take on a student unless the latter displays great resolution and energy in his inquiry. This is technically called Great Faith. After some time the disciple's hidden doubts and reservations appear in the form of a crisis, generally centring round some point of the teaching or some action of the teacher. When the problem fills all the waking hours without a moment's forgetfulness the stage is called the Great Doubt. The working of the mind ceases. Finally there is a flash which is called in Japanese satori or Realisation.

Classically satori was once for ever, but in later Zen, especially in the Rinzai transmission, special methods were used for bringing about the Great Doubt more quickly. The disciple was presented with a ready-made riddle, generally one which had formed in the mind of a disciple in the Tang dynasty, the golden age of Zen in China. The advantage of the ready-made riddle, or Koan as it is called, is that crystallisation of the pupil's doubts takes place more quickly; the disadvantage is that the crystallisation, not being spontaneous, may be incomplete, and then in spite of a satori experience the process must be gone through again with another Koan. In the life of Hakuin (in the Yasenkanna section of this book) we see a number of crises, some centring on a Koan and others spontaneously arising on the classical pattern. Teachers of the Soto transmission of Zen do not make so much of Koan technique.

This technical point explained, the texts here translated can speak for themselves. I am grateful to Primate Takashina and Abbot Obora for Zen instruction and for permission to translate from their writings. My thanks also go to the Japan Broadcasting Corporation for the stills from their documentary on Zen. Dr. E. Conze very kindly read the manuscript and made some valuable suggestions. Two or three of these translations have appeared in the English Vedanta magazine *Self-Knowledge*.

Part One

On the Heart Sutra

by Abbot Obora of the Soto Zen Sect

*The load of ignorance
makes footsteps of evil*

When the Bodhisattva Kannon was practising the profound Prajna Paramita wisdom he saw all the five aggregates to be Emptiness, and passed beyond suffering.

'O disciple Shariputra, form is not different from Emptiness, Emptiness is not different from form; form is Emptiness and Emptiness is form; and so also with sensation, thinking, impulse and consciousness. All these things, Shariputra, have the character of Emptiness, neither born nor dying, neither defiled nor pure, neither increased nor lessened.

'So in Emptiness there is neither form nor sensation, thinking, impulse nor consciousness; no eye, ear, nose, tongue, body nor mind; no form, sound, smell, taste, touch nor object of mind; no element of eye, nor any of the other elements, including that of mind-consciousness; no ignorance and no extinction of ignorance, nor any of the rest, including age-and-death and extinction of age-and-death; no suffering, no origination, no stopping, no path; no wisdom and no attainment.

'The Bodhisattva, since he is not gaining anything, by the Prajna Paramita has his heart free from the net of hindrances, and with no hindrances in the heart there is no fear. Far from all perverted dream thoughts, he has reached ultimate Nirvana. By the Prajna Paramita all the Buddhas of the three worlds have the utmost, right and perfect enlightenment.

'Know then that the Prajna Paramita is the great spiritual mantra, the great radiant mantra, the supreme mantra, the peerless mantra, which removes all suffering, the true, the unfailing. The mantra of the Prajna Paramita is taught, and it is taught thus:

Gone, gone, gone beyond, altogether beyond,
Awakening, fulfilled!'

1. THE IMMUTABLE SCRIPTURE

A word on the full title of the Sutra, which is Maha-Prajna-Paramita Heart Sutra. The first three words are Sanskrit, *Maha* literally meaning great, *Prajna* meaning wisdom and *Paramita* meaning having reached the farther shore. Maha here has the sense of ultimate, and Prajna means wisdom in the Buddhist sense, namely negation of all things, not the little intellectual wisdom of the world. So Maha-Prajna means: by the knowledge of ultimate Emptiness to make all things Emptiness. Through the power of the great wisdom, which makes absolutely everything Emptiness, to cross over to the other shore –Paramita.

When it is said to make everything Emptiness, what is meant is human life, our actual life in society, with our crying and laughing, elation and sorrow. In Buddhism this life is called the world of birth-and-death. Buddhism is the desire to make this world Emptiness and to live, as far as it may be possible, without holding anything in the heart, in Emptiness. To seek to do that, to become like that, is the manifestation in the heart of the power of wisdom, the power of knowledge of ultimate Emptiness.

Through the power of ultimate Emptiness to cross to the other shore – this other shore is called in the Sutras Nirvana. Nirvana is the farther shore, and the world of birth-and-death is this shore. From the present illusory reality let us make the crossing to the shore of realisation of Nirvana. Throughout Buddhism the idea is to cross from here to the beyond, to transfer our living from here to there.

All Buddhism, Mahayana and Hinayana alike, has the notion of passing over. It is in Zen also. Passing over does not necessarily mean being reborn in the Pure Land paradise in the west; it means to pass from the present illusory I to the I of the bliss of realisation. The idea is a very sound one, but people today are not interested in being reborn. Instead they talk of living meaningfully, of how to live. But in their talk about how to live there seems to be a frank spirit of doing it at others' expense, which is hard to justify. Religions which look at life on the basis of distinction between oneself and others always have this sort of exclusiveness of spirit.

The object being a rebirth of the I, Buddhism is of course extremely introspective. How can the I progress from the world of illusion to the world of realisation? The basis of the process is self-introspection, self-reformation and thoroughgoing training. This is the passing over, this is the rebirth, and the idea runs through Buddhism. In whatever scripture you look you will find it, and not only in the Heart Sutra.

The word 'heart' in the title of the Sutra means the essence. Into a mere 264 words has been condensed the immense Great Prajna Paramita Sutra with its sections. So this little Sutra is called the heart. The Chinese character for Sutra (which is read in Japanese kyo) was selected by the first translators because it has also the meaning of eternal, and the sense is that the Sutra is an eternally immutable truth. All the teachings of the Buddha are given this appellation kyo, and from ancient times to the present, and from the present into the future, never do they change. The Heart Sutra is one of them, being the essence of the Great Prajna Paramita Sutra.

Consider our life as it is with its crying and laughing. There is in each case a trace left; of crying it is a trace of crying, and of laughing the trace of that laughter. Our living leaves these traces. What I emphasise always is that even when it is laughter, we should laugh with a truly empty heart. But we never do so. 'Cold today!' and 'Well, how are you?'–remarks which have no point, poured out like oil and accompanied with a little laugh. No real laughter of pure enjoyment, because even in our laughter the heart does not become empty of its burdens. The thing called the I is in the breast and the laughter is centred round that I. It is laughing because things seem well for the I. And the crying is of the same sort. With each step the track is left, and this way of life is the world of birth-and-death, the life of illusion.

THE LOAD OF IGNORANCE

The tracks left by joy or grief are footmarks. In religious terms, Zen master Dogen calls them the heavy burden of ignorance, root of evil. Though I die, the roots of the evil I have created are not annihilated. When he calls it a load, he means that all the time in our progress through life there is a great burden which is more than we can really bear, and shouldering it we are drenched in sweat, until finally our human life ends. We long somehow to put it down, by some means to lighten ourselves of the weight of conceptual thinking; but to do so we have to be earnest seekers. If we are not, there is no religion. The quest for inner lightness – to be able to cry but with an emptiness within the heart, to laugh but with the same emptiness – such is the great wisdom. To do things with an inner emptiness is the wisdom of the knowledge of ultimate Emptiness. The power of negating into emptiness is the great wisdom.

Only by completely negating our human living through wisdom-power is realisation of the far shore possible. This is the Prajna Paramita. Only by ultimate Emptiness can we live each step of this frustrating life without a load on the heart, only then sport in the world of satori called Nirvana. Nirvana is translated 'extinction', but what extinction means is that even when crying the crying leaves no traces. Similarly, Emptiness does not have the meaning of a void with nothing in it. It means not leaving a track. At present each step is leaving a track, but if we can realise this trackless state, even in the present life, it is Nirvana.

To sum up: we are to pass over to the Nirvana state which leaves no track, by the power of the ultimate Emptiness of the Prajna Paramita wisdom. The way to do it is set out in the Heart Sutra. The practice is to cross to the world of Nirvana by the power of wisdom, and to train the heart to do it is what the Heart Sutra teaches.

2. THE CIRCLE OF LIFE

When the Bodhisattva Kannon was practising the profound Prajna Paramita wisdom, he saw all the five aggregates to be Emptiness, and passed beyond suffering.

Now we begin the text. The Bodhisattva mentioned is generally known as Kannon, though sometimes as Kanjizai. In either case the first character of the name, Kan, is seeing, and it means to see things as they really are. To see things as they are gives freedom, and so the Bodhisattva is called Kanjizai, the one whose sight is freedom.

If asked what Buddhism is, I say: 'Buddhism is seeing everything as it really is.' Seeing the real form of everything is Buddhism. We don't see the real forms; we think we do, but in fact we don't. When we consider the I, whether it is something lasting or not, outside Buddhism they always presume that the self must have a form. They make it something quite definite. But in fact it is an error to think there is a permanent self which we can call I.

But they make the basic assumption of a lasting self, and then through education they come to think of it as something absolute, and most people think that self-development is the aim of education. If we go deeply into the question whether the I is after all really existent, we shall find that it is not. The conviction of an existent I, a superimposition of what is really non-existent, is called in Buddhism clinging illusion. Once having taken the non-existent as existent, on top of it we construct the worlds. On the foundation of a non-existent I there are laughter and tears, joy and sorrow. This is the basis of all errors.

But the Bodhisattva Kannon sees the true form of every-thing. That true character is the character of Emptiness. We call our I what is ultimately an empty form. The Bodhisattva has freedom because his wisdom pierces to the true form, and so he is called the Bodhisattva of freedom.

The true form is Emptiness, is no form. True form is no form. The Bodhisattva of freedom realises the form of no form in everything, and this Bodhisattva realises the no form, the principle of ultimate Emptiness, particularly in sounds. So he is often called Kannon or Kanzeon, namely one who perceives the sounds of the world.

Now there is Kannon in the hand, for instance, and then again in the eye, and so it is that the Bodhisattva is called thousand-armed and thousand-eyed. They represent him with a thousand hands and a thousand eyes. Elsewhere it is said that he is all hand, that he is all eye. But although his power of penetration and freedom works in everything, it is especially in regard to sounds that his virtue is manifested, and so he is named Kanzeon, he who perceives the sounds.

Human life can in fact be considered as sound. Mostly human nature expresses itself in sound. A man's whole character is revealed in his voice. There's a saying that if you get a man to open his mouth you can see his insides, and it is true that you come to know a man's spirit, his inner nature, if you make him say something. So it is that nothing is so important as what we say. When there is harmony in the intercourse of words, the household will be at peace. And mutual harmony in speech is the first manifestation of peace. Such is the importance of sound.

Kannon Bodhisattva is a being who has emptiness within the heart whether crying or laughing. On a happy occasion it is felicitation from the bottom of the heart – but within is emptiness. We wretched people don't do that. On the lips are congratulations, but in our heart –'Curse you!' We have no freedom of sound, no spontaneity in our words. Holy Kannon has always emptiness in the heart whether in joy or sorrow, and so he has freedom of mind. It is the power of ultimate Emptiness. In the negative sense it is Emptiness, but in the positive sense it means that in our crying or laughing, body and mind are one. This is the true spontaneity of speech. When our words are directed to freeing others and freeing ourselves, the grace of Kannon will be in that place.

The Bodhisattva attained the state of power and freedom by practice of the profound Prajna Paramita, the practice of ultimate Emptiness. When it is said 'profound', it has the meaning of complete. To penetrate deeply, deeply through our everyday life, and by the power of negation to obtain freedom. Negation means the complete negation of our living.

In the Nirvana Sutra is the illustration of three animals crossing a river, and they represent three ways of living. The animals are elephant, horse and hare, and they illustrate shallow and profound views of life. The hare slips along on the flotsam on the surface, and such is one who sees only the surface of life, and this only of the physical form. The horse crosses by swimming, half immersed in the water. Such goes a little deeper into life. The elephant forges steadily across with great strides along the bottom. This sort of living is! going right into life and penetrating to its real basis, and it is complete living. In the Nirvana Sutra the elephant crossing the river stride by stride is the illustration of completeness in living.

Now the hare is the symbol of taking life as the body. Such thinking is always escapist, it is the psychology of the shirker. The shallowest view of life is to consider it something which can be evaded, to think that one can escape by moving from here to there. This is the superficial attitude of hoping to get out of our responsibilities. I have my role in life, which may be a labourer or a cleaner; my allotted part was that of a priest. Each has his own; to be a religious is also a role. And I sometimes wonder whether the role of a religious man is not rather an unworthy one. Among religious people I am of no account, but, even so, I always seem to be getting pushed into things by flattery.

All the time one is being flattered. 'No one but Your Reverance... please may we have a few words from you ...' One gets caught and there's nothing for it but to comply. One cannot help a feeling of being pushed into things. Oh to find some way to give it up and retire, buried snugly in a temple in the country – such thoughts may come. And yet, those who refuse to follow the flatterings, they are awkward fellows too. The fact is that everyone does act at the instigation of others; even such a great man as Saigo was flattered by others into doing things. And to follow the flattery and try to do what they want is all right, but in any case, however flattered, we don't escape our role in life.

To switch from role A to role B, from B to C, from C to D, in the hope of peace and happiness, is an attitude of evading responsibility. Not liking the life of a priest, let me have a go at business, and if I don't like that I can try a Government job ... so I try to get out of my obligations. The one thing I don't want to do is my allotted role. Evasion of responsibility is the most shallow attitude to life.

The second attitude is typified by the horse. Here the idea is to reduce life to a void, to emptiness, whereas the first attitude was to run away from life, from the responsibilities and inconveniences of family and so on. This second attitude goes somewhat deeper. They think that if this unsatisfactory human life can be reduced to emptiness, it can be done away with and got rid of altogether. In Buddhism this is called the way of the Second Vehicle. Those who practise the Hinayana (the Small Vehicle called the Second) are termed Shravakas and Pratyeka Buddhas. To their way of thinking, this life of birth-and-death is altogether emptiness, and Nirvana is the state of literal annihilation. Not to be born again, not to come back to this world, to annihilate the individual completely, a literal annihilation of body and mind, is their state of Nirvana. This second attitude to life is that the sorrows and joys of life are all to become nothing.

The third is the Bodhisattva's view. Evasion and escapism were the attitudes of the ordinary man, who always wants to get out of his allotted role in the world. He thinks if he can get out of the present condition there will be satisfaction just over there. But the third view of life is to find the meaning in this life, which however much we try to escape we can never escape, and it means to realise the true Nirvana state. Escapism is the first attitude. The second is to think that Emptiness means neither to weep nor smile nor do anything at all. But life is not like that. We set ourselves not to weep but life brings us towards tears; we set ourselves not to be angry yet anger rises – it cannot be escaped. The third attitude, the profound attitude, is spiritual practice to discover a power in the very midst of the sufferings of life. Profundity means technically to penetrate right into life.

The Bodhisattva Kannon, having practised the profound Prajna Paramita, penetrated to the true world of Nirvana in the midst of life, the life which cannot be evaded however we try. In Buddhism another word for life is the wheel of birth-and-death. A wheel once set going continues to turn, so it is a symbol of life. 'Turning' is an important idea in Buddhism, and there is no Sutra which does not refer to it. Our heart turns, impelled by some force, and that impelling force is very mighty. In a great flood, bridges, houses and everything are carried away, and the vaunted human strength becomes a tiny thing in the face of the power of nature. Admittedly in a certain sense man does conquer nature, but really the word 'conquer' is a complete misnomer. Man boasts that he conquers a mountain or something by his human strength, but in fact he is the conquered one, he is always subdued.

How ridiculous to speak seriously of conquering a mountain! Idle good-for-nothings use such phrases, but far from being conquerors we find them nothing but a nuisance to the world. The impelling force of which we spoke is the force of nature, and against it our human strength can at most offer a limited check or resistance, for the time comes when its might is irresistible. That force is turning the wheel all the time, and this is called revolving in the six worlds.

The wheel has the heart at the centre, which is the heart of clinging attachment to selfhood. Self does not exist, but cling-ing to a non-existent self is the centre on which the six worlds are upheld.

Of the six, the worlds of the Asuras, the heavens and the worlds of men are the good and the worlds of the animals, hungry ghosts and hells are the bad. We speak of our allotted place, but the truth is that it is not allotted to us by any God or Buddha. Buddhism does not speak of position as allotted by a God or Buddha. An allotted state is spoken of, for want of a better figure, but in fact there is no allotted state. Buddhism does not teach that God created the world or created man. This life, which cannot be got out of however we try, is not imposed on us by God or Buddha. Our present state has been raised up by each one of us on the delusion of the mind called sticking attachment to self, thinking what is not self to be a self. The worlds are created, and they are self-created. The six worlds are upheld by the delusion that something exists which is non-existent.

Even those called good are good worlds but still based on sticking attachment to self. Good and bad alike are all relative states upraised on attachment to what is called self. Good which is based on attachment to selfhood is a state which still leaves considerable track of impurity. And of course evil leaves a great track. While illusory clinging to self is not completely destroyed, the worlds of illusion, whether good or evil, are upraised thereon. So the good is not complete good, it is all with the idea of getting something out of it. 'If I do *this* then I shall get *this*, and if I do *that* then that...' It is in the expectation of results. It is a good, but with oneself at the centre. For example, I set out to take some cakes as a present to a neighbour, which is a fine thing to do. All would be well if I made the heart empty and forgot the fact that I am doing a good action. But I won't do so. 'Here I am carrying sweet cakes and by and by there be a return...' That's the way the thoughts go.

People these days talk about sacrifice, about self-denial, about service, but as it is all based on attachment to self, quite soon they are expecting to see some result. So it is a mean impure good, though good it may be called. After all, then, what is regarded generally as good is still a mean thing, and what to say of the evil which leads to the evil states? Until attachment to self at the centre melts, while the heart deluded by an I is not completely negated, good itself is an illusion and evil also. While the illusion remains unbroken, the so-called good, founded on self as it is, only by chance does any real good. We do some good, but by accident. Suppose, in the role as a priest, one is teaching people. Because the role in which he finds himself happens to be good, he is doing some good. We say he does the good, but in fact, because of the part he is in, he has to do good whether he wants to or not. Again they say of a religious man that he's conscientious. But that conscientiousness of his is nothing. It's just that the part requires it and so he has to be like that. The kindly and devoted teacher is in a role where he has to be kindly and devoted, and so he is kindly and devoted. Anyway, a bit.

What I always say to schoolteachers is this: 'You are teachers and I'm a priest; kindly and devoted both of us. We have got to be. But if the conditions were unfavourable we'd quite likely be manifesting as demons or hungry ghosts or animals. We ought to find some other condition which is not moved under any circumstances, don't you think?' While the illusory clinging to self is not negated, while the so-called without-I or Mu-ga is unattained, then it just depends on the environment whether we happen to be doing good or happen to be doing evil. In Buddhism the eternal meaningless round, always on the basis of illusion, is called the six worlds. Isn't that our life, the round of the worlds, happening to do good, happening to do evil – again and again the same things? Perhaps we are good now, but when the evil associations chance to rise, We begin to do wrong. Where is there security? If we just follow the associations, doing good or evil as chance has it, how can our footsteps ever be firm? Isn't it just a pointless circling round the circumference of the wheel? The other day I saw in a newspaper that a graduate of the Women's Teachers' College had killed her stepchild. She was quite a figure in education, and yet when for a moment she met with bad associations she did that terrible thing.

So however much we try we can never escape from the worlds of good and evil which are constructed on our attachment to self, unless we smash this wrong clinging. The worlds are built by ourselves, and so we cannot escape from them. This inescapability is called the Wheel. The wheel of birth-and-death is to be caught, turning in pointless repetition, forced to move though reluctant, impelled by the great and terrible force which Buddhism calls karma. We are driven by the force of our previous actions; our whole life is impelled by that karma. Suppose I go to the house next door determined to keep calm and exchange a friendly greeting. But I find the neighbour's attitude insulting and shameful, and finally the karma bubbles up and I have become angry. Where does it bubble up from? However I try to suppress it I can't. By that great force is our life moved each instant.

Someone presses a banknote on one – 'Go on, take it!' It's not altogether an unpleasant feeling. Of course one ought not to take it, but in a poor priest like myself there is a little impulse to stretch out the hand. The karma of receiving bubbles up. All of this is from the heart; on the heart are constructed the worlds of good and ill and the karma which has built those worlds, past and present, is moving them. However I resolve not to be greedy, my greediness appears. However I resolve not to be angry, my anger rises. Our human life is such that however we resolve not to weep over things, we come to the state of weeping.

We can't finish with this life. The spirit of Mahayana is to find the truth in each step of it, in anger itself to see Emptiness, in the very complainings over our lot to know the profound Prajna Paramita.

THE REAL MEANING OF NEGATION

The Heart Sutra teaches us the method of training by which we can see Emptiness in each one of the steps which, whatever our attitude to life, we are being forced to make. At present we keep doing the same things over and over again in the endless round of mundane good and bad, built up on the ego illusion. We may happen to do good, we may happen to do evil. How could such a great man do something so strange, how could such a man do something so wrong! ... This is all part of the round.

Step by step retreading the same paths, impelled by the deep-rooted karma, such is our life. The spirit of Mahayana Buddhism is to discover life's real meaning.

Against our will, anger rises. To discover in the very midst of it the world of light is the meaning of the phrase 'the passions are the Bodhi'. Profundity means (technically) to penetrate to the real form under the illusion, the truth in all the lies, and when the true character of the self is realised in the religious sense, that is the knowledge of ultimate Emptiness: a fire to negate everything.

The profound Prajna Paramita negates self. In Zen, negation means to drop, to throw all away. By this power of renouncing, the power of the knowledge of ultimate Emptiness, we complete a training which carries us across to Nirvana. Master Dogen says: 'Just discard and forget body and mind, and throw them into the abode of the Buddha; then following the movement of the grace of the Buddha, without use of force or fatiguing the mind, leave birth-and-death and be Buddha.'

The important thing is to see right through to the reality of the illusory self. This is why body and mind are to be discarded and forgotten. The Zen way of meditation is renouncing. Renouncing itself has to be renounced, and so it is no renouncing. Religion is not something imposed. The effort to throw off body and mind has to be renounced, and so it is no renouncing. Not renouncing, and yet not without renouncing – that is the real renouncing. It is not something done at the instance of another.

To look through to the real form is to penetrate to one's reality, free from self-deception. This is the true renunciation; not trying to throw away, and yet throwing away all the same. When we can gaze steadily at our ignoble self and understand, this is itself the principle of renunciation. When you really come to a deadlock, it is renunciation. To change our condition from this to that is not renunciation, which never implies switching from A to B. When there is complete realisation of the true character of one's self, there is a feeling of throwing the self away, and that is the principle of renunciation. When we have penetrated to the bottom of this illusory self, not without negating, and yet not negating, there is the power of the knowledge of ultimate Emptiness and the self is thrown aside.

Through the power of ultimate Emptiness, of renunciation, there can be a change to a state which leaves no track. When self has been thrown away, when the discipline matures, there is a crossing to Nirvana. This is the method of the practice of the Bodhisattva Kannon.

AN ILLUSTRATION OF THE WHEEL

Long ago in China lived the poet Sotoba,* who speaks of his own experience in the poem:

> In two years transferred through three provinces,
> I grow old without regret:
> Round and round like an ox
> Step by step treading the old footmarks.

In a bare two years to be transferred three times is not pleasant, but it happens even to a man of rank so high. He was probably transferred as prefect. Gradually he grows older, but though not especially regretting that, he sees in his life the image of the ox, going round and round endlessly like that ox working at the grain mortar. In ancient times the farmer used an ox

* Su T'ung Po. Except for familiar words like Tao, Chinese words are given as the Japanese read them.

to work the mill. Pulling at the mill it would pace round and round times without number, going round ceaselessly, never knowing any end. It is just like us – yesterday too we were happy and sad, laughing and crying, and the day before just the same. Ten years ago it was the same, twenty years ago the same. Step by step treading the old footmarks –our present actions are no more than retreading those old footsteps where we trod before.

But Sotoba's point is not simply this being dragged along and nothing else. He is not the man just to be dragged help-lessly along. What is this dragging? It was explained before how by the force of the past karma one becomes angry though resolved against it, how one's cravings arise against one's will. All are dragged by their past karma. Just to be dragged along means to be sorrowful when it is sorrow, to laugh when it is laughter, to be angry when it is anger, to clutch when it is craving. But there is nothing in that sort of life, and it is not Sotoba's point. He is hinting at a training which reveals a real meaning at each step. We ourselves, however we try not to be pulled, cannot help it. Still, I who yesterday was just pulled helplessly along, today come to hear of the Buddhist teach-ing, and now in each step as I am pulled I find a world of true illumination. In this is the glory of Mahayana Buddhism.

THE TRUE CHARACTER OF THE SELF

What then is our life of endless circling? It may be the mind arising beautiful as heaven, it may be the mind springing up as a hungry ghost; but both equally uncertain, because we have still to circle in the worlds of good and evil.

A SECOND ZEN READER

I am asked to speak before a congregation. I make my address just like a Jizo Bodhisattva, with the feeling that there is nothing in my heart. By the power of the knowledge of ultimate Emptiness, I speak in the Nirvana state, with nothing in the heart. And those who listen also are in the Nirvana state with nothing in the heart. They are like Kannon Bodhisattvas.

And yet – this Jizo of mine, and those Kannons of theirs, are surprisingly unreliable. One day, when roused by some association, this Jizo becomes furious and looks like a hell-mask, and those Kannons put on the face of hungry ghosts. Life is so uncertain: where can we find a firm footing? Human life is always quivering with uncertainty. When the circumstances are good we do a little good, and when they are bad we may do anything ... painfully the uncertainty of life is borne in upon one.

For some three weeks out of each month I am away from the temple. I am not often home, and so when I do come back I send a postcard two or three days beforehand, saying exactly what time, to the minute, I shall be at the tram-stop. Then I anticipate that I shall be met. The day comes. In the train I have a pleasant feeling, with nothing on my mind. And in the tramcar too there is the feeling of emptiness, my mind clear. Someone will be meeting me. I descend at the stop and look around, look everywhere, but no one has come to meet me. Not a soul ... and where has gone the pleasant feeling, where has Jizo gone, where has faith gone, where has satori gone? I hardly ever get home, and I told them the exact time, and however busy they may be surely someone could meet me? These ignoble hell-feelings arise. This is the simple truth. However I try to suppress them they will not be suppressed.

Such is the truth of one's delusion of self. Why didn't they meet me? I try to suppress it but I cannot, and that is the manifestation of what we are. Having done a little spiritual training in my life, I scold myself at making all this fuss in my heart over nothing at all, and pick up my bag and walk back to the temple. As I come up to the gate someone comes out. 'I was just coming to meet Your Reverence, we got your postcard with the time, but there was an emergency suddenly, so please excuse us...' And greeted by his smiling face this abbot's hell-heart disappears. Why, of course, how natural it was! And I feel completely happy and content. The heart revolves endlessly. Suddenly angry, suddenly at peace, where can one find a firm foothold?

Going in I call: 'A cup of tea, please.' 'Why yes, we have been expecting you and the water is on the boil!' I feel more and more pleased. Nowhere like home.

But perhaps it isn't like that. When I get to the gate, no one comes out. More and more annoyed I go in. 'Bring a cup of tea' – my voice is as yet quietish. When there is no answer I call again, my voice a bit louder. Still no answer. Now I am shouting: 'Aren't you bringing that tea?' Isn't it pathetic? As I have shouted, so now there is a shout back: 'Com*ing*!' It is a row already. In that 'Com*ing*!' are a million shades of meaning. While the cat's away we were getting on nicely and now the old man's suddenly come back and as usual there'll be a fuss over every little thing, he's so crotchety. It's all in the 'Com*ing*!' I have caught it and cannot take that one word calmly. Suppose the tone was bad, yet is not the relationship of teacher and pupil most close, a relationship that cannot be severed?

And in the homes of the world, isn't the parent-child relationship similarly close? Though the children answer rudely, though the disciple answers rudely, ought we not to be unmoved by it? I preach about human conduct, and I am supposed to be practising spiritual training, am I then so pitiable I cannot swallow one word without an upsurge of anger? When I am brought to penetrate to the truth of that I which is the truth of my self, when I realise what the self really is, then renunciation appears of itself and there is already freedom from the body and heart.

By the profound Prajna Paramita we penetrate to the bottom of life and know the truth of our selves, and then we cannot help renouncing. When the discipline has been done, crossing into the world of Nirvana by that renunciation, I see the world of liberation is already here.

3. AWAKENING TO THE CHARACTER OF OUR INDIVIDUALITY

He saw all the five aggregates to be Emptiness, and passed beyond suffering.

This is illumined vision, seeing things as they really are. Satori is when the real character of everything is seen. When renunciation of self is complete, the absolute, the state free from all conditions, in which at present we are putting our faith, will actually be realised. The world of faith is to act entrusting all to Kannon. Religion is not logic and all that. To entrust all to Kannon means to have merged self in the state of Kannon. By the power of my self I can do nothing, not even check one tear or one impulse to anger, but when I have pierced to the truth at the bottom of that self, the holy form of the Bodhisattva Kannon appears, which rescues the I into the absolute unconditioned. Surely this is the true world of faith also.

Faith is not just worshipping Buddha, but rather realisation of the truth of one's self, Zen master Dogen is always telling us to learn how to withdraw by turning the light and shining it back. This light, this illumination, is the radiating mind, the mind released towards objects. When a sound is heard, the mind is released to that sound, we are attracted by the sound. Or, when a form is seen, the mind transfers to it and we are attracted by the form. The light, the mind which is attracted to objective things, we are to pull back, and the training of the Zen school is this withdrawing a step and considering. What after all is this anger, this impulse to greed? The first condition of spiritual training is to withdraw and come to realise the truth of one's self. He speaks of withdrawing, not of advancing; it is the meditation of withdrawal which is important. There are different currents in the one Zen sect, but the doctrine of the Master Dogen is indeed a true doctrine. To go charging headlong to another place cannot be called training. Today people are apt to be hotheaded in rushing around. Perhaps some of them think that life is an arena of competition and this charging about is the thing to do. They have the impression that they need only discard all human illusions and charge forward to conquer everything, and so sweep all before them in the human arena.

But the method of Buddhism is not like that, not just rushing out to objects. Its basis is at every step to withdraw and realise fully the truth of what is called self. The trick of withdrawal is the basis of the Buddhist training.

When the truth of selfhood is known, the world of faith manifests clearly, that faith which entrusts everything to Kannon. It is illumined vision, and with it comes the entering into faith, namely realisation. When the life of faith manifests, it is the life of satori. He who enters into the state of faith is one who verily has entered the state of satori. He is awakened. And then, the I who was saved soon becomes the I who saves. I who was saved by Kannon, who was merged in the world of liberation, am now no different from Kannon. Saved by Kannon, that one becomes holy Kannon, and must now be active for the salvation of all. Saved by Kannon, merged in Kannon, being Kannon, is the state of satori and awakening. The state of entering faith and the state of satori cannot be different. The meaning of illumined vision is that the saved must soon become the saviour; the state of awakening is that the self saved by Kannon must become Kannon. It is in this that satori must reveal itself. The condition of entering faith, of enlightenment, of awakening to the truth about one's body and mind, is the realisation that the five aggregates are all Emptiness. Enlightenment is fully grasping this. Hitherto the five have not been Emptiness, but now there is a clear understanding of what they are.

THE NATURE OF INDIVIDUALITY

Now what are these five aggregates? Roughly speaking, our body and mind. In Sanskrit the aggregates are called skandha, which means a heap or bundle or collection. According to associations of karma, form (Rupa in Sanskrit), sensation (Vedana), thinking (Sanjna), impulse (Sanskara), and consciousness (Vijnana), these five collect and integrate to make a body and mind. Our body and mind come out of them. In other words, they stand for our individuality, and to awaken to what that individuality is, is illumined vision. When the nature of our individuality is clearly seen by us, that is awakening and that is illumined vision.

First of the aggregates is Rupa, and the sense is solidity, in other words materiality. The whole material world is in Buddhism called Rupa or form. Form thus means substance characterised by impenetrability; substances cannot be in the same place at the same time. They mutually obstruct each other and are impenetrable to each other. Our body is material and impenetrable and so it is called the form-body, and this is the technical Buddhist term for the body of flesh.

Second is Vedana – sensation. This can be treated as an operation of the mind, though technically it is not classed under the mental functions. (The next one, Sanjna or thinking, is a mental function. In the Hinayana doctrine there are forty-six such functions of the mind, and of them the strongest are listed separately.) Vedana is represented in Chinese by a character which literally means receiving, and it is the function of the mind by which everything is taken in. The function which takes in the things, whether they be long or short, however they may be, is this Vedana.

Sanjna means thinking, in notions, in ideas. As Sanjna, things that have been taken in are recollected, and this is the function by which there is attachment to them. Such is the function called thinking. The strongest factors in deepening illusory attachment are these two, Vedana and Sanjna.

Fourth is Sanskara which has the meaning of construction and changing, but these are used in a technical sense and the general meaning of the Chinese character is action. Here however it is action of the mind, the character having in Buddhism the significance of mental action, with no question of speech or outer activity. This one word takes in the whole condition of the mind.

So construction and changing means from one thought to the next, thought by thought, constructing the varied karma in the wheel of birth-and-death. In the mind we are creating the various karmas and constructing distinctions: 'I try this' and 'I try that'. Such discriminating is the way the mind works, and this is what Sanskara-impulse means. Under it are included the remaining forty-four out of the forty-six mental functions.

Fifth is Vijnana, with the meaning of the consciousness which determines things. It is also called the mind-lord, and as such determines right and wrong, good and bad consciousness, the mind-lord, has the function of determining as right or wrong, good or bad, everything that has been taken in.

Form then is the physical body, and the other four are mental functions and the mind-lord. This body and this mind, one skandha-aggregate and four skandha-aggregates, which by the power of karma have temporarily come together, we call individuality. Now a temporary combination of form and mind, namely the five skandhas of Rupa and the others, is not a definite real entity to be acknowledged as 'I'. It is something which has only temporary life, and so is nothing actual and real to be taken as I. Yet by the force of beginning-less illusory attachment, attachment from long long ago, it is taken as a definite self. Clinging tenaciously to this is called the condition of the delusion of the five skandhas – it is thinking something to be which is not, considering what has arisen from temporary association of the five aggregates to be somehow a self. This empty fancying is just like creating in a dream the various forms which rejoice and grieve.

Yoka Daishi says: 'In dream clearly are the six worlds seen.' When we see a dream clearly there are the six worlds, with their sufferings and joys. While seeing the dream we do not think aside that it is a dream, and so we are pursued and sweat in agony. When we know what the dream really is, there are no six worlds, but while seeing the dream there are for me the opposed sets of good and bad. The five skandhas are all delusion. The five are not something definite and real, but our delusion is that we hold tenaciously to them as being an actual and real self.

For this reason in the old translations the Sanskrit word skandha was translated by a Chinese character which means to conceal by covering. The skandhas are the delusion which covers the true nature, the absolute, and does not reveal it. The form of the absolute is, in a word, no-form. The real form of everything is obviously not in fact any definite form, but by the force of the delusive form of the five aggregates, our absolute no-form appears as a form. The doctrine of the five skandha-aggregates indicates self-delusion.

DELUSIVE ATTACHMENT TO SELF

Consider for example a madman. He does not know he is mad: when he realises it is madness, soon he recovers. These days there is an increase of the madness which affirms its own sanity. To be saying one is sane is already madness. He who says 'I am mad' is indeed the real man.

I knew an abbot, extremely straightforward by nature, who, as it chanced from his karma, went out of his mind. He was so honest, it seemed that his very honesty drove him out of his mind. He was in a country temple in Mino, and the monks were anxious about him and came with him to Tokyo. I was at that time in charge of a school and they came to ask my help. I put him up in a little room in a small temple, and then took him to the hospital.

We all went along together, but when we came to the hospital he would not hear of going in. 'I've come to Tokyo to see the city,' he said. 'As these monks here can tell you, I have never had even a cold in my life. It's nonsense for you to ask about my going into hospital, ridiculous, I'm perfectly well.' It was very awkward. But in such cases a lie is permissible. 'Of course you are! Very strong, and nothing wrong with you at all. And the thing is, that there's a health investigation going on, and it's people who aren't ill and who've never had any illness that they want to examine; they want to have a demonstration of perfect healthiness. Luckily you have come to Tokyo for sightseeing, so you won't mind just being examined in the hospital, will you?' 'Oh, if it's just an examination, all right,' and he went in.

The head of the hospital made his various tests, and while he was running through them the abbot was saying: 'Doctor, I'm not ill and have never had even a cold my whole life long.' The doctor was saying with a faint smile: 'No indeed.' The patient was mentally sick, but when he asserted he had no illess the answer could only be: 'No indeed.' Tell the madman he is mad and he does not understand. If he could understand, he would be well again. Are not the people today all raving and yet bragging of their sanity?

The five skandhas have no fixed real nature, and in relation to our body and mind we are as if dreaming or raving when we take them as somehow an actual self.

Then what is this I? This I is a madman. It is clinging to empty delusions in a dream. When by good fortune through the holy teaching we realise little by little that the dream is a dream, that is joy. Still seeing the dream, still raving, yet more and more realising the character of life, that it was a dream, was a dream – such is real happiness.

In each one of his works Master Dogen says: 'Those who would practise Buddhism must deeply deeply feel the passing nature of things and have faith in karma.' in the opening passages of his book on spiritual practice he says: 'The heart which feels the passing nature of things is called the Bodhiheart.' He is urging us to feel impermanence and to believe in karma; first the round of impermanence, and then the principle of karma. The round of impermanence is seen by reviewing our past, looking back over tens and tens of years; the principle of karma has reference to our actual present experience.

LIFE IMPELLED BY KARMA

When in tranquillity we consider ourselves, the first thing that comes up is the problem of the flow of time. Through time we feel impermanence. Fifty already, sixty already – in these terms we reflect on the past. When we see young people we think how we ourselves were young and how we can never, alas, return to that time. Well then, let us return you to your youth, say about twenty, but under one condition. And it is: that you will have to relive your life once more in exactly the same way. So now we return you to your youth, but with this condition. Well? No! I *do* like to be young, but to live it all over again, I couldn't stand it.

When young, life seems like a level flat highway. As the years pass, it is not like that. Diving through waves great and small, assailed by storms, I scrape through up to the slope of the sixties and now to the seventies. To repeat again this life of turmoil, that I should not like. Someone has said that life is a tightrope from cliff to cliff across a valley filled with up-pointed swords. Well, if so, I have just managed to get through the sixties.

On that tightrope moreover we have to perform stunts as we go along, and my stunt was to be a Zen priest. I was not much of a priest, but that was the trick I performed.

Performing our various stunts, we have scraped through so far, but it's a life that makes one shudder at the thought of going through it again. When I think how it would have been better not to have done that, and as for this, if I had done it I should have fallen into the sword valley and perished – truly I should not like to live it through again. How do you feel? Never mind going back tens and tens of years, I don't want to have last year over again. I don't want to have yesterday again. I don't want to repeat, and the reason is that my life never had any meaning that was a meaning. If it had had a real meaning, I shouldn't mind reliving it. But when I think of the life I have lived, in which the Buddhaheart never at all manifested, a life passed pointlessly, I do not want to live it once more.

Then they come and tell us that Paradise is on the Other Side, so perhaps we want to hasten forward to that glorious Pure Land? Here again I don't feel much like it. What, don't I want to get to Paradise quickly? No, not too quickly. There is a story about an old woman who used to pray very earnestly in the temple every morning. The abbot overheard her one day: 'I am getting older and older and the children and the grand-children are too much of a trial. The family are so quarrelsome and I've no more interest in staying in this world. I pray that Your Grace take me to you soon' – all this from the bowed head. He thought he would see whether she really meant it or not, so he hid one day behind the Buddha image. The old lady came as usual and unsuspectingly prayed her usual prayer to be taken soon. The abbot shouted: 'in answer to your prayer

I am going to take you now!' The old woman shrieked, 'Won't the Buddha let me make a joke!' and fled.

Every day we are making such jokes. If we were taken now, we should be aghast. All the time it is like that. There is a Pure Land, but as to going there, we are not ready yet.

So it is that I do not want to return to the past, nor to hurry to the Pure Land which soon awaits. Not to hurry forward nor yet to go back. Then how should we go in life, day after day? Not merely days, but at each step, let us be neither hastening forward, nor retreating.

Why do we suffer in life? It is just because we are simply being pulled along. Each step is a compulsion. In the Bodhi-heart chapter of the Shobogenzo classic, Master Dogen says: 'From this body to the intermediate state, and from the intermediate state to another body, all moment by moment are changing. In this way unwillingly impelled by karma, the wheel of birth-and-death revolves without an instant's rest.'

By force of karma made in former lives all are helplessly going over and over the round and never stopping. The force is karma: irresistibly impelled along, praying to become without-I and yet unable to be without the I, so I am pulled by it.

The world for which we pray is called in Buddhism Mu-ga or without-I. All seek somehow to live without an I, not to have an I in the heart, to live from the bottom of the heart. But there I am, in spite of my prayers, unable to be without the I.

My prayer is for no great thing. I always pray just that, with the hundred-and-fifty-odd families to which I minister, I should live in peace in a state of no-I. But it does not turn out so. One family who were very hospitable to me – I say hospitable, but this is the country so it means a radish or a carrot from time to time – well, they were hospitable ... Then the grandfather died and they asked me to perform the funeral rites. When the day came the rain was falling in torrents and the roads were flooded.

A servant came and told me he had been sent to take my things, including the ceremonial chair and the umbrella which are used in the rite. With kindly intention (and make a note of the kindliness of my intention) I said: 'On a day like this they surely won't have the funeral rite in the open, so there is no point in your struggling through the storm with that big chair. Please just take my things. For a chair, they could ask the school next door to lend one and I use that for the ceremony.' The coolie happily agreed and went off with just the bag.

I followed a little later and came to the front door, imagining that it would obviously be held indoors. The young master was standing at the door with a countenance like thunder. 'Your Reverence, we are not going to have the funeral ceremony.' I had a sinking feeling that something was wrong. 'Not going to have a ceremony for your grandfather ...but why?' 'Never mind why, but we've cancelled it.' What to do? 'I can't think what might have made you cancel it. Now tell me what it is that has happened.' 'Abbot, it's no use pretending you don't know!' 'Pretending? I'm not pretending about anything;

please tell me what it is.' 'All right then, I will. This morning we sent a servant who was to ask to take your chair. And what did Your Reverence say? That the chair would get spoilt if he carried it through the rain. So we've asked such a mean priest for grandfather's funeral that he won't risk spoiling his chair, and we were going to have grandfather saved, but now we're not going to and the ceremony's off!'

When this sort of thing happens, where is the no-I which we are always thinking about in our heads? Where is the satori? It is not easy when one actually comes up against life. Where is that faith and enlightenment which were here just now? And what remains in our heart at this moment? However I pray to be peaceable, when such unreasonable accusations are made I want to shout: 'Shut up!' But I cannot. Let the abbot think. If I give that shout, am I not doing something which I shall never be able to retrieve? That is in another part of my head. I want to shout, but our life is this, that one cannot shout. We are impelled on the wheel of birth-and-death, borne along on the round of karma; and for all my prayers inevitably my character appears, the illusory character appears. However I pray to be without I, my character is that I cannot be without I, and as I come gradually to comprehend this I cannot help feeling an inexpressible loneliness and desolation.

I do not know how much you feel it, but in the contradictions revealed by introspection there is a great feeling of desolation. This contrary life in which we cannot be what we like to be, when examined from within, produces a desolation.

Even with one's parents, unable to discard the meanness of self; even with spiritual people, unable to throw off our deceits. Yet when I come to penetrate to the very bottom of that desolation, then, as I stand, there suddenly manifests a power of absolutely unconditional forgiveness. It is a power which will never desert man. Impelled step after step as we are in the circling of this life, in which when we want to speak we cannot speak, that power of absolute forgiveness is dimly glimpsed, and then a joy comes to the heart. 'It was wrong to have caused you anger – but for the sake of your grandfather who has just died, will you not let me take the funeral service?' To be able to say these words from the bottom of the heart is through no power of my own, it is the joy of the grace of Kannon. When the self seems merged in Kannon, enveloped in the power of absolute forgiveness which is Kannon, for the first time the heart becomes empty. If all I can manage is: 'Well, let's pass it over; let me take the service,' then the joy is only a faint one.

Some people dub it self-intoxication, this spiritual joy. When conditions are favourable (they say) you experience a feeling of well-being within. So they say, and let them say it. I have the deep certainty that it is an ecstasy, something blessed, and the joy comes when the speech proceeds from a heart which has been emptied.

'The five skandha-aggregates are emptiness.' It means that the illusion of the five is only an illusion, and when attention is directed to the true character of the self, beyond the feeling of isolation I suddenly find myself embraced by that power absolute, and enter the world of salvation, of awakening, of satori.

ISOLATION FROM OTHERS

I have described realisation in terms of isolation, but it does not mean the isolation of separation from others. *That* isolation comes from being deserted. 'I am old and the family don't want to talk to me now; how lonely I am!' Such is the isolation of being separated from others.

When I go to a house, as I arrive they say: 'This way, Your Reverence, go right in, right through,' and they take me to the reception room. It seems like a great honour, but if you ask me I must say that it is no honour at all; it's just that hanging about the living rooms the old man will be getting in the way so it's 'this way please' and I am tucked away safely.

It is a loneliness, to be pushed into a corner. When I come to a house I should like to talk to the young people, but I'm not allowed to and am tucked away without meeting them. This is the loneliness of isolation from others.

The old lady of the house doesn't enjoy being told: 'Granny, today we are spring-cleaning so you sit in this corner and rest.' She feels how she is getting old and being pushed to one side. Instead if they say to her: 'Oh, Granny! There's no one who can do over the best tea-things like you . . .' then she feels it is so, and does them with great satisfaction. This is the way to understand old people.

So the loneliness of isolation from others is the feeling of having been deserted. There is a longing to be appreciated, and when this is cut off the loneliness is unutterable. As I see it, our whole life is a demand to be appreciated. Everyone, young or old, is seeking to be understood. Our life is a quest for someone who understands us, and when the sought-for understanding is cut off, what a bitter feeling it is!

These days there is talk about the deadlock in thought and the deadlock in economics; but in one sense the frustration is the perpetual cutting off of the understanding sought by each one. On this frustration arise all the manifestations of deadlock. In frustration and deadlock we are bound to feel loneliness at being isolated from others, at having been left behind by the world.

But then there comes a reaction to the loneliness; there is a karmic reaction in a desire to find light, in a conviction that there is still one way remaining open. And it is to confront directly our true nature, and in the deeps of the inner isolation to find that one power absolute.

FORGETTING SELF

The Buddha did not have the loneliness of being deserted; he knew the loneliness of having a million friends. It is said that he renounced his home when he was twenty-nine –in one tradition, nineteen. Before that he rejoiced in his beautiful queen and his lovely child. He excelled in learning and wisdom and was a master of all the sciences and arts. As the heir to the throne of the emperor, he was held in great honour. At no time were the circumstances ever lonely. He was one who had satisfaction in all the desires of human life. There was no outward isolation.

Inwardly it was that he felt extreme loneliness. In spite of all the wealth and talents and accomplishments, when he considered that the self could rely on none of these things, he was overwhelmed by unspeakable loneliness, and this was the loneliness of the Buddha. So his renunciation of everything and his withdrawal to the mountains alone for his spiritual practices were not from outward loneliness but the loneliness arising from inner awakening. When he penetrated to the very bottom of it, he touched that supreme power of absolute compassion.

What can a poor mortal say of holy Kannon? Only that Kannon too is one who once pierced to the bottom of the inner loneliness, and, realising liberation, turned to the universe with the conviction that all others must be saved also. The ideal of Kannon is salvation for oneself and for others also.

That being of the world of faith and satori, namely the state of Emptiness holding nothing, who weeps with me and laughs with me, is none other than the Bodhisattva Kannon. To carry all beings beyond suffering is the vow of the Bodhisattva. This life in which weeping we must not weep, laughing we must not laugh – even while we are treading the agonies of the wheel – is the world of liberation of holy Kannon. Nay, more, is it not in the midst of the pains of life and death that we experience more and more deeply the Buddha power of holy Kannon?

Next in the Sutra comes the declaration to the disciple Shariputra: 'Form is not different from Emptiness, Emptiness is not different from form; form is Emptiness and Emptiness is form.' Such is human life as seen by holy Kannon; when it is said that form is not different from Emptiness and Emptiness not different from form, it does not mean to sweep away completely what is called form and to take up something separate called Emptiness. On the contrary, through the form-body of illusion, the body which is revolving in birth-and-death, we are to make Emptiness and embody the meaning of Emptiness. Emptiness does not mean a void with no content.

4. THE TRUE CHARACTER
OF THE HUMAN SELF

'O disciple Shariputra, form is not different from
Emptiness, Emptiness is not different from form; form
is Emptiness and Emptiness is form; and so also with
sensation, thinking, impulse and consciousness.'

Here Buddha, as holy Kannon, tells to Shariputra, highest
of the disciples in wisdom, the true character of life. Form
is not different from Emptiness and Emptiness not different
from form, and so with Vedana-sensation, Sanjna-thinking,
Sanskara-impulse and Vijnana-consciousness. These are the
five aggregates as explained before. The full reading would
thus be: 'Form, Vedana, Sanjna, Sanskara, Vijnana are not
different from Emptiness, and Emptiness is not different from
form, Vedana, Sanjna, Sanskara, Vijnana.'

Form means the form-body, namely the physical body. The
other four are taken as mental functions of the mind-king; taken
together they are mind or spirit. With the physical form come
together here in temporary association through karma, we speak
of our individual nature. But in it there is nothing like an essence
of permanent nature. There is no permanent I. Our deep-seated
delusive involvement in the notion of a permanent I, somehow
existing in this temporary conglomeration, is called hanging on
to self, and the five skandha-aggregates are a synonym for our
sticking to self, which manifests as the passions. The movement
of the mind under attachment is called passion.

Specifically the passions are greed, anger and folly.
To covet what should not be coveted, to be angry at what should

not cause anger, to say foolish things for which there is no ground – these are the activities of our heart. Such activity, based on attachment to self, is passion. It manifests physically as word and deed: our illusions become apparent in our words and actions.

Form is not different from Emptiness. It is not said that if forms are negated we shall get Emptiness. The character of the skandha-aggregates is the character of Emptiness. The illusion as it stands is wholly of the character of Emptiness. Through the very existence of attachment to self, more and more deeply we can come to appreciate a taste of the world of Emptiness. In the illusory form – body in the round of birth-and-death, let us by realising Emptiness grasp the real meaning of Emptiness, that it is not a void without content.

PASSIONS ARE THE BODHI

In his Discourses at Eihei-ji Temple, Zen master Dogen says: 'When the clay is plentiful the Buddha is big.' By clay he means the raw passions. The mental operations in the mind within us which seethe and rage unbridled – these are the clay. And the more abundant it is, the greater the Buddha into which it comes to be moulded. The stronger the force of attachment, the greater the Buddha which is made.

'Do you ever get angry?' 'No, I'm never angry' – such people have nothing *to* them. When the time of anger comes, when the whole body is ablaze with it, then it is that the form of the Buddha must be seen. By coming to the taste of Emptiness in the midst of illusion of the five skandhas, we really grasp the meaning of what Emptiness is. In the Vimalakirti Sutra is the phrase:

> In the soil of the high meadows, the lotus never grows; In base slime and mire does the lotus grow.

These are the words of Vimalakirti expressing the truth that the passions are the Bodhi. He is saying that the passions are the Bodhi, that birth-and-death is Nirvana. The lotus of course is the sense of having entered into faith, of having realisation. On the high ground we cannot find that lotuslike state of satori. The lotus is a beautiful flower, and surely should grow in the dry clean soil. But as a matter of fact it does not grow high and dry in the pure soil of the meadow.

What is the mental state symbolised by the meadow? I suggest the following for consideration: In the heart of a man of elevated views and penetrating intellect, there is hardly either entry into faith or satori. As a rule in what they call their study and so on, it is all simply thinking as an intellectual operation. By means of intellect, the Buddhist ideals of no-I and Sameness are built up just as concepts, and people who think they fulfil themselves through these artificial concepts never have faith or realisation. I believe that a world of concepts, where the no-I or Sameness are only things thought in the head, and where there is no effort at spiritual practice, is an empty ideal. It is only something thought about, and so it is an empty ideal which has no content. It must be admitted that those who think themselves fulfilled through the ideal of a void like that, have in fact no passions. They do not suffer from the passions of life. But since there are no passions, naturally there is no bodhi-awakening. Believing their nature fulfilled by mere pictured concepts, they have of course none of the sufferings of life. And as they have no sufferings, they cannot experience the real bodhi-awakening.

THE CONCEPT MONSTER

The so-called no-I of people like this, which is built on concepts, is no more than the no-I of a child. In an ironical sense one could call them good quiet people. Happy people!

It is a widespread aberration in our thought today that many think self-completion is attained by concept-building, and fail to make any efforts towards the ideal. Even among Zen aspirants are numbers who fall into the same error. 'Lying on the face or sleeping on the side, I have freedom...' they quote, and think that getting up just when one likes is enlightenment there and then, and that the state of satori is to express everything just as it comes. 'Oneself a Buddha and all others Buddhas'; so thinking, he is sure he is already a Buddha.

There are some middle schools which profess adherence to the sect of Buddhism of which I am a priest, and at one of them I used to give instruction. The subject was Morals, and the talk had to be based on the Imperial Rescript on Education of the great Emperor Meiji. I found that however sincerely I spoke they never listened sincerely but used to drop off to sleep or start whispering to each other. I realised that to go on talking about ethics and morality in this way was having no effect at all.

So one time in a fourth-year Morals class I came down from the platform and said: 'Today I'm dropping my position as teacher and you are going to drop yours as pupils, and I want you to answer me a question straight and without feeling you have to be polite. My question is this: in the syllabus there must be subjects that interest you and subjects which you like least, and I want you to tell me honestly which they are.' Nobody said a word. I repeated my question and finally one clever boy said reluctantly: 'Well then, I will answer the teacher as he asks. In our syllabus subjects like Maths and English are difficult, but the more you do of them the more you find in them and gradually they get quite interesting. But you, teacher, come here just once a week for one hour and you talk about national morality, loyalty and filial piety all the time, and it's the most uninteresting subject. Couldn't the Morals class be taken out of the syllabus?'

I was forcibly impressed by these words out of the mouth of a child. The Rescript is a reflection of the character of the great emperor, but we teach nothing of his great character, nothing of his life; the Rescript has become no more than a concept, thought about logically in the head. There was no life in what I was saying and so there was no reaction from the pupils. Rather natural, one might say.

I remember once asking a man who was a big name in the educational world: 'What is the foundation of the nation's morals?' and he replied at once: 'Why the Rescript on Education of course.' What a forlorn answer, wasn't it? The Rescript is always kept tucked away on the highest shelf. Now when religious people talk about religion today, when Zen priests talk about Zen today, I'm afraid it tends to be like that.

It is shameful how without touching upon the sublime life of the Buddha, Buddhism is simply presented as spun out of our own heads. What relevance will that Buddhism have to life? For it has never had any life in it. The basic error of the intellectual is to think that the aims of Buddhism are elevated views and penetrating intellect, and that these things in themselves be a fulfilment of human nature.

I believe this is what the Vimalakirti Sutra means when it says that the lotus is not born in the soil of high meadows. The lotus of faith does not bloom in the heart of the man of elevated views, nor is there any satori there. His non-egoity is a conceptual non-egoity, and it can be compared to the no-I of the child.

THE NON-EGOITY OF THE CHILD

Someone has said: 'The heart of God is the heart of a child.' In a way it is true that a child's heart is pure and free from malice, and we can also call him Mu-ga or without-I. But we cannot say that this no-I of the child is the Mu-ga of the Buddha; it has to be admitted that it is not the non-egoity and freedom from malice of the Buddha. We must be clear on the point. Take for instance this poem:

The infant step by step is attaining wisdom:
Alas that he is also moving away from the Buddha!

The child is indeed free from malice and he seems pure, but gradually with the years he advances in the wisdom of all the goods and bads and rights and wrongs. Sad it is that through this he becomes estranged from the Buddha. And so – he must return to that long-lost child... But when we say that, do we really mean it? In a sense the child certainly is without-I and seems pure, but in fact it is not so. It is a Mu-ga of escape from the sufferings of life, a purity which knows nothing of human sorrows, whereas the Mu-ga of the Buddha comes forth from out of that suffering.

What is human suffering? It is our worldly ties which torment us on account of mistaken sticking to selfhood. A state of no-I, when by not accepting those ties we escape from them, can perhaps be called purity. But it is not the true Mu-ga. It is an unconscious state, and the state of the child is in fact an unconscious state.

Unconscious here means that the self is not connected with the world of others. The false sticking to ego is not yet cognised, the thought 'I' has not yet arisen. Our thought of I arises on the basis of consciousness, but in the state of infancy the sticking to egoity has not yet appeared in consciousness. So it is not a state of no-I but rather a state of no-consciousness, namely a world of instinct. It is the pure instinctive world which is the world of the infant's no-I. When he wants to cry he cries, when he wants to laugh he just laughs, and that is his world. He acts by instinct. Since he has not yet any attachment to ego, his world is simply things as they are, and there is no mud of ties of passion. But neither is there the lotus of Bodhi.

A neighbour made a present of some very delicious cakes to a certain family. He gave them to the little boy. It so happened that an important guest came on a visit at that very time, and the mother wished to make use of the cakes to offer the guest.

But the child, to whom they had been given, resisted the proposal. 'They were given to me and it's not fair to give them to an uncle from somewhere...' and finally the mother had recourse to a lie. 'They are yours, but please just lend them to Mummy to put before the uncle. The uncle, you know, is a perfect gentleman who would never take one. When he's gone I will give them back to you.' 'Well, if it's only lending...' and the cakes were taken and laid before the guest. Now as it happened this man was unusual in that he did not drink rice-wine at all, not even a drop, but he had a great liking for sweet things, and between sips of tea he began on them. The little boy had stationed himself at the crack of the door, and saw the uncle, who was not supposed to eat anything according to what he had been told, take one and then another. He managed to hold himself in while the fourth cake went, but at the fifth a howl burst forth: 'Mummy, the uncle's eating all my cakes!'

Is this no-I? Is it purity? If this sort of no-I is the life of Mu-ga taught in Buddhism, then it will be destructive of society. And so we can see the child is neither pure nor without I. It is simply that he has not yet risen to consciousness of individual selfhood. "When they talk of returning to the state of a child it is not really returning to childhood that they mean; if you did return, what would it be? The no-I of the child is not the real no-I but no-cousciousness. His world is the world of unalloyed innate instincts, of responding to their drives. When he wants to laugh just laughing, when he wants to cry just crying, such is the world of the child. And in that happy-go-lucky state there are no ties but also no Bodhi. In this sense we should understand the Vimalakirti Sutra.

People today follow their whims and think human life can somehow be fulfilled by so doing. They think the point of life is this laughing when the innate impulse comes to laugh, and crying when it comes to them to cry. Those who think the thing is to express the impulse as it comes have in a sense the no-I of children; cynics call them the bread-and-butter of life, but the truth is that they are simply happy-go-lucky.

THE WORLD OF LIBERATION

To be brought to the full realisation that this form of clay is the form of what I call my self, is a great blessing. My tears are born of sticking attachment to self, my laughter is based on sticking attachment to self, all my passions are on the same basis. This form is of clay. I have accepted the burden of taking that form as my true form, but then there dimly comes the perception of dropping of self, a sense of the grace of the Kannon of self-submergence, a state of emptiness with no burdens. The joy of it is not that a lotus has grown out of the mud, but that the mud as it stands has become a lotus.

From the mud of sticking attachment there is experienced indescribable bliss; from the five skandhas of illusion arises the state of awakening called Emptiness, where there is no burden on the heart. The five are not different from Emptiness, and when we can see the false attachments as false attachments, more and more we experience the world of liberation called Emptiness. It is not that false attachments are swept away and then some world of Emptiness appears; nor is Emptiness the world of the I just as it stands. Emptiness is not the I which just cries and just laughs. Our human life is to want to laugh but to be unable to; gradually we come to realise that life is just this wanting to do something but being unable to do it.

I remember going to an anniversary day at a girls' high school, whose headmistress knew me well and had asked me to speak. After the formal ceremony, I mounted the rostrum to address the four-hundred-odd pupils. Their united gaze fixed itself on me standing there. Some of them hardly knew what a Buddhist priest looked like, and now one stood before them, and they wondered, I suppose, what on earth I was going to say. As they stared at my face, one of them giggled. That alone would not have mattered, but her neighbour took it up, then a third and more and more till the whole hall burst into laughter. The most brazen-faced must have been taken aback – how could one make a speech?

I cried in a loud voice: 'This is a happy time for you. It is the time of flowering! Your faces are beautiful like flowers, but that is not the only likeness. For now, when you want to laugh you can just laugh. When the thought just comes that I look funny, you can laugh. Whenever you want, you can just laugh as much as you like. And this is the time of being flowers. When you want to cry too you can cry – that is what it means, the time of flowering.

'But as you grow up, see how it is. When you get married, though you would like to laugh, if your father-in-law is there you have to suppress it, and you have to hold it in in front of other relatives. The day will come, won't it, when you'll want to laugh but must not.'

'Now is it happiness just to laugh and cry when you want, or is it happiness to want to cry and not be able? Is it happiness to express one's feelings just as they come, or is it happiness to want to express them and be unable to? Which is happiness? For you that time is surely coming, and it is through that time, by experiencing that frustration of life when you want to laugh but cannot do so, that you come to know of the liberation taught by the Buddha, absolute freedom from conditions. That I, which in crying yet does not cry, in laughing yet does not laugh, is realised as one's form and that is the state of liberation.' And so my speech was made.

The abstract terms of the Heart Sutra are a little difficult. Twice is used the phrase '... not different'. The first instance was: 'the forms are not different from Emptiness'. But the world in which the self of the five skandha-aggregates does not recognise its sticking attachment to self is not, as it stands, Emptiness. What brings us to see the false clinging attachment to egoity as a false clinging, and perceive in the depths our true character, is the state of liberation called Kannon. It is submerging the self in the emptiness in the depths of the heart. And so form is Emptiness, and through the existence of forms we come to give them their true meaning as Emptiness.

POWER TO CONDEMN, POWER TO CONDONE

The world of Emptiness is not some world without crying and without laughing. Emptiness in the tears themselves, Emptiness in the smiles themselves – this is the real Emptiness. Then the phrase is turned round: 'Emptiness is not different from form.' When with all my might I plunge what is called my self into the heart of Kannon Bodhisattva and in that heart become completely naughted, then the laughter and weeping called form can for the first time have a meaning. Only as Emptiness have the forms their great meaning.

'Now, just for today let me try.' And then at the time when I wanted to burst forth like a thunderstorm, when I wanted to rage with the anger erupting in me, 'just for today' – and somehow I realised this blazing up for what it is, something which is blazing up, and then there was a taste of the state of liberation. That I was enabled to speak for that moment with the ill-feeling vanished from my heart was no power of mine. It is the power of Kannon. Through Kannon's grace there comes a breath from the absolute: Emptiness is no different from form.

Form and Emptiness cannot be separated however much one tries, and the life in which they are reconciled, the life of Kannon, is expressed in the next two phrases: 'form is Emptiness, Emptiness is form'. Form here stands for all five skandha-aggregates. The power which simply negates them is, 'form is Emptiness'. It is not only illusory clinging which is negated; the real Emptiness is negation of what is called Buddha also. The power of the negation begins with the five aggregates but goes on to negate all. Only thus is the world of supreme wisdom and light hinted at. It breaks the illusory clinging to self and goes on to negate even the Buddha form. If it stops short at the Buddha form, it is not Emptiness. 'Form is Emptiness' points to the state of ultimate negation. Only when there is that absolute negation the next phrase be manifest – 'Emptiness is form'; the affirmation of all conditions. Because there is Emptiness there can be form; therein is manifested the compassion of Kannon.

It is to be noted carefully that in this Sutra the phrase 'form is Emptiness' comes first, and 'Emptiness is form' comes afterwards. In the Diamond Sutra similarly the world of negation comes first and only then the world of affirmation. It is after absolute negation that the so-called world of unconditional affirmation appears. The first phrase, form is Emptiness, means 'this will not do, and that will not do' and never gives assent. Then comes 'this will do, and that also will do', which is the world of Emptiness is form, of affirmation of everything just as it is. First the power to condemn and then the power to let be, but these powers to condemn and to condone are never separate from each other.

On each side of holy Shaka is an attendant: one riding a lion, with a sword, who is the Bodhisattva of wisdom, and the other on a gentle white elephant with a lotus, the Bodhisattva of compassion. They express the Shaka in the middle. Holy Shaka is the power which when it is time not to allow will refuse to allow and refuse to allow and always refuse, with the sword of negation. Yet he also has the power of infinite forgiveness. The power of tolerance and the power of negation are not separate, and Shaka symbolises the human life in which these two are merged. When we prostrate ourselves even a little before holy Kannon, there comes first 'form is Emptiness'. When we come to see in serenity how our delusions do not amount to a self, that is form is Emptiness. This not amounting to a self is the so-called discarding of selfhood. It is the world of Emptiness, absolute selfnegation, absolute throwing away of self. And at the bottom of that negation of self is experienced the world of holy Kannon – who however deep our sins will never turn away – the world of profound affirmation, the world of permission. Kannon at the time of condemnation will condemn and condemn without any limit, and at the time of condoning will pardon and pardon without any limit, and this is the Bodhisattva Kannon.

I remember how I felt when I was forty-four and my old Zen teacher died. When I was young I used to be scolded by both my parents and my teacher, but now my parents had come to praise me up and never scolded me any more. It was only the teacher who still had a harsh word for me, and when he died an inexpressible loneliness came over me.

Four years previously I had gone back to my home town, and I used to act as his assistant. At that time I was fairly full of myself: quite a name in Buddhist scholarship, they said, and then I had been a professor here and a headmaster there – oh, I was pretty well satisfied with myself when I came home. I was one of those men of elevated views. I came home with the conviction that my wisdom was very far-seeing. But the teacher still saw me as the same runny-nosed youngster as before. Every day I used to scrub the floor, and the teacher would come up behind me: 'Look at that! What sort of cleaning is that supposed to be? All black-and-white patches like a picture or something. The number-one boy ought to be able to make a better job of the cleaning than that!' Another time when I was supposed to have made a reply in the wrong tone: 'If you still don't know how to answer properly, your spiritual training doesn't amount to much, does it!' I was scolded over everything.

I remember one day an old lady came to the temple and told us she had brought the girl along with her. On asking how old the latter might be, she said: 'Oh, she's sixty!' Certainly, to an old lady of eighty, the daughter of sixty is still a girl.

In spite of all the wrinkles, a girl is a girl; whatever the age may be, a girl is still a girl. In the same way, to the teacher I was still a little boy. However distinguished a countenance I had put on, however many professorships I might have held, that was nothing to the teacher. I might feel myself a man of elevated views, but the teacher's comment was: 'If you still don't know how to answer properly, your spiritual training doesn't amount to much. Do some self-examination!'

Sometimes I used to feel: "Why doesn't the old man let up a bit, yes, let up a bit, just a bit, damn it! But when he died, I had that unutterable loneliness. Now there are many to praise, but the teacher who was really kind to me, who used to hide his tears of love under his scoldings, is dead. And I am alone.

Holy Kannon is one who looks on all as his children, and shows compassion to all, whatever they may do. We have to face the fact of our illusions. We must realise our clinging attachment to the five skandha-aggregates for what it is. In this, he negates and negates. But when we come to realise we are nothing at all, then we have an experience of the sublime world of Kannon which embraces all in an infinite forgiveness. In the Bodhisattva the world of Emptiness and the world of form are not two; form is Emptiness, Emptiness is form – in these words the Buddha speaks of the state of the Bodhisattva Kannon.

In the Genjokoan book of Shobogenzo it is written: 'In the feeling of inadequacy of body and mind the dharma is fulfilled; know also that in the feeling that the dharma has been fulfilled by body and mind, there is yet something lacking.' When we come to know of Buddhism, to feel that it is well, that all is at peace, to set ourselves down in a state of so-called satori, means there is as yet no real understanding of Buddhism.

If we are really receptive to Buddhism, there is always the feeling of not enough, not enough; limitless endeavour and striving continued age after age, that must be the spirit of Mahayana. There is no feeling of completion. Not enough and still not enough – gradually self is negated and the world of liberation reveals itself.

5. TRANSCENDENCE

'All these things, Shariputra, have the character of
Emptiness, neither born nor dying, neither defiled nor
pure, neither increased nor lesssened.'

These phrases addressed to Shariputra teach the character of Emptiness. As Emptiness, it can have no characteristic form. We may think that even in Emptiness some form must remain, but there is no need for it to be so. The form is no-form. The form of the true Suchness is the form which is negation. True form is spoken of as the form of no-form, and only so can it be expressed. That form is nothing visible to the eye. It is the life of truth. The whole spirit of the Heart Sutra is that the real form, the form of Suchness, is no-form, and so it is said here.

'All these things' means the five skandha-aggregates. We are to discover the satori of Emptiness in these illusory forms, to awaken to the fact that the forms are at the same time Emptiness, and then there is no more the form of birth-and-death. The standpoint here is that the world of birth-and-death is just illusory sticking to self.

By the time we have the thought that something has come, it has already vanished – such is this world. The worlds of relative good and evil – of hell, ghosts, animals, Asuras, men and also the heavens – are all upraised upon illusory sticking to self. When we think we have done some good, that good is at once destroyed. It is all appearing and vanishing.

Because these worlds stand on illusion, even good is no more than an occasional event caused by associations, and when the associations are bad the manifestation created by that good entirely disappears. Relative good and evil are always appearing and disappearing. A Sutra says: 'Though merit be piled up high as the Himalaya, one flash of anger and it is all consumed.'

Merits from good deeds, when associations become a little unfavourable, are destroyed with the flaring up of passion. Our life is destruction of what has been built, and building up of what has been destroyed; underneath building a destruction, and underneath destruction, building – repeating again and again the same sort of things. All worlds of illusory attachment to self are the same.

This pitiable human state is symbolised in the Buddhist story of Sai-no-kawara. In the ruined temple of Daisenji there is a representation of Sai-no-kawara of which a good deal remains. There is the dry river-bed of the story, and in the middle stands a great stone figure of the Bodhisattva Jizo. Around it have been piled up countless little pagodas. The story is familiar to all Japanese: how those who die in early childhood go to this place and employ themselves in building the pagodas. They remember their parents in the world, and build one for their father and one for their mother, piling up the stones one by one. A demon suddenly rushes in from the side, and whirling an iron pole smashes down everything they have built. The children, terrified, run to the stone Jizo and hide themselves for a while in the long sleeves of his compassion.

We get the feeling of pointlessness, that it is futile to keep building up the stone towers only to have them smashed down by the demon. If they are always to be destroyed, why build them? But that will not do, for this is Sai-no-kawara, a place where the karma associations find fulfilment.

When the demon goes off, the crowds of children come out again and build their pagoda towers. Just as they think they have finished, out comes the demon and all is destroyed. What was built up is broken down, and then what was broken down is rebuilt. Repeating again and again the same task is the state of Sai-no-kawara. Is not our human condition like that also?

In the worlds of relative good and evil raised up on illusory attachment to self, we may do some good, but then when the karma associations are unfavourable, evil passions arise and destroy it all. We rebuild what was destroyed, and what we build is again destroyed. When we think we have completed something it disappears, and what has disappeared again comes about – so the endless wheel of life revolves. This is the character of the human condition, and in spiritual training it is called the law of circularity. 'What a thing to happen to such a splendid man!' This is all the shiftings of human nature. From the point of view of spirituality, it is only going round and round in the world of relative good and evil. It is not the profound spirituality. All the worlds of illusory sticking to self are worlds of birth-and-death.

THE WORLD BEYOND BIRTH-AND-DEATH

When Bodhidharma first saw the Emperor Bu of the Ryo dynasty, the latter was such a devout Buddhist that he was called the Buddha-heart Emperor, who would surely be the one to hear the true tradition. The Emperor asked: 'Since ascending the throne I have built and endowed temples, distributed the sutras and supported monks and nuns; what has been the merit?' He inquires what merit there is in these things. Bhodidharma answered: 'No merit.' There is no merit in them – what a bleak reply!

Buddhist priests nowadays don't say such things. When the people contribute their tiny coins and ask: 'Your Reverence, is it meritorious?' we only say: 'Merit without end!' But Bodhidharma did not say that. No merit, was his reply, and the Emperor now asked: 'How so, no merit!' The great teacher, feeling the pathos of the question, told him that there was a little something – 'There are small fruits on earth and in heaven resulting from impure seeds, but it is like the pursuit of shadows and in reality nothing.' 'What you have done has some merit, but it is no more than chasing a shadow. It is not the real merit of true Suchness. For building temples and supporting their monks and distributing the scriptures are all only the world of good which is upraised on the I as the centre. By accumulating merit of this kind you will be born in heaven, because the good deeds were done in the expectation of a result. Small fruits on earth and in heaven, on the self as basis. The seeds of good actions aiming at such fruits are always polluted. It is planting impure seeds, contaminated with passions.

Impurity is passion. It is the impure feeling which comes of sowing seeds of good actions in the deluded passionate heart, in the expectation of securing results. Good which is based on illusory attachment will one day inevitably fall, as the associations come up, to the evil worlds. It is not the real good, that is what the great teacher meant.

'Then what is real merit?' pursued the Emperor. Bodhi-dharma said: 'As pure wisdom, holy and perfect – something empty and pure; as such it is not to be sought through the wisdom of the world.' The real merit is the wisdom of absolute ultimate Emptiness. It is complete and without defect and absolutely empty and pure. So it is not a thing at all. You cannot find it by seeking with the wisdom of the world as you are trying to do. It is the Emptiness which the Heart Sutra indicates to us: 'O Shariputra, all these things have the character of Emptiness.'

With the taste of the wisdom of ultimate Emptiness, the bottom of the heart becomes empty, and the characteristic of Emptiness is to find that sublime flavour, that direct experience, at each step in our path of illusory good and evil. It *is* this step after step, this being helplessly pulled along. In step after step, as we are impelled by our karma of good and evil, we experience the world of the true Emptiness and purity.

If we gaze at that feeble good of ours, we shall find even there the world of liberation. If we look at that feeble evil, even there the form of Emptiness appears. This present I, which builds but under whose building there is destruction and destruction, which is helplessly pulled along, must awaken to Emptiness, and when the bottom of the heart becomes empty the actions are based on Emptiness. Now it is not a world of birth-and-death called good or evil; the feeling of doing and building does not arise, and so there is no birth-and-death.

The patriarch Dogen says in his Shobogenzo: 'If you think of following the way of the Buddhas and patriarchs, have no expectation, no seeking, no clutching; without purpose pursue the way of the ancient sages and tread the footsteps of the masters.' It is without purpose and therefore without thought of result. Throw right away the idea of acquiring merit and follow the words and footsteps of the ancient sages. Such is the way the Buddha-children are to follow.

In the state when there is Emptiness in the depths of the heart, there is no building up at all, but in compensation there is no knocking down. It is just because we feel something has been built that there is a corresponding destruction. 'O Shariputra, all these things have the character of Emptiness, neither born nor dying'; and this is the experience of reality without birth-and-death.

There is one little thing to add. When there is building up through impure goodness, in that very impure goodness let us try to establish the world of Emptiness. And when there is breaking down through ignoble evil, in each moment of that breaking down let us try to establish the great world of Emptiness.

LIVING HAND-TO-MOUTH

'Neither defiled nor pure.' These are clearcut words. In the world of Emptiness there is neither the so-called impure ordinary man nor what is called the pure Buddha. It transcends values, goes beyond price-setting. When we say ordinary man and sage, we are in the world of values where there are ordinary men and there are sages. Our life is all comparative values. What is his standing? What is he worth? – always on the basis of status. People are accorded standing on the basis of their value. That one has the standing of cabinet minister, that one of prefectural governor. This is the world of values.

Zen master Dogen warns us: 'He who is truly called a teacher must not lack the power to stand apart from rank, and must have the spirit of transcending distinctions.' He must abandon considerations of rank and distinction, and unless he has the power and spirit to do that, he cannot be a true teacher. Caught in the toils of values, no one can be a true teacher.

The ranks from which he must be able to stand apart include the ranks of ordinary man and Buddha. So it is that Emptiness is called holding nothing in the heart, carrying nothing whatever in the heart, not even the thought: 'I am a Buddha.' The Buddha is one who has thrown aside even this.

When the Buddha says he is a Buddha, he does not place himself on a higher rank. The real Buddha forgets the Buddha-form and merges himself in the bloodstained world of living beings. He does not glance down at living beings from an elevation with consciousness of superiority and address them: 'O ye dull deluded ones!' Merged in this our world of defilement, melted into the heart of the people and forgetting his own form, such is the Buddha who has passed beyond the world of values.

There was a family in which the grandfather and grandmother used to go regularly to the temple. But the rest of the family were heard saying aside: 'They've gone to the temple and now they are Buddhas, but from morning to night they are so fussy about every little thing. Buddhas in the house are a real nuisance!' That sort of Buddha is truly a Buddha-burden. To feel one has attained quite some faith, quite some enlightenment, and from this higher level to look down on the others and speak – those people are real Buddha-burdens. They are Buddha-illusions. The Buddha of Buddhism has forgotten he is a Buddha and throws himself into the heart of all living beings. He is one who lives hand-to-mouth without care.

A Sutra describes the life of Buddha: 'Verily the wooden man sings, and the stone woman rises to dance ... as if a god, as if a fool.' Becoming a man carved of wood he can sing songs, becoming a woman of stone he dances a dance. Wooden man and stone woman have transcended value. As we are not wooden men and stone women, we feel that even in our singing we must do it at all costs well, and our dances must be properly executed. And yet we become more and more incapable at them.

The words 'fool' and 'god' have not here their usual meaning. Fool here means one who follows everything, who goes with everything. For the sake of fools, becoming the heart of the fool – this is going with things. With clever people becoming the heart of the clever, with each person becoming what that person is, and speaking from the bottom of the heart, such is the Buddha. Seeing we are formed of illusory attachments, for the sake of this wretched sinner he becomes the heart of a wretched sinner and there speaks – that is the Buddha.

'Ye are the good, therefore come ye here, and ye are the wicked, therefore go ye there'; so to divide the people is not the Buddha. Becoming the heart of each whatever he may be, from the bottom of the heart, throwing away Buddhahood, he speaks.

There is a phrase from a Sutra: 'For the child's sake, forgetting.' In bringing up a child, incongruities are forgotten. Seeing the baby about to walk but unable yet to do so, the mother takes its hand. 'Here we go, aren't we clever not to fall!' she cries as she staggers along with tiny steps. She feels with the child and forgets how comical she looks.

A boy of five was sent to board at my temple. Bringing him up from that age, I used to think of myself as a parent to him, and he used to get round me. I would tell myself that as an adult I must not spoil him, but the fact was that having brought him up from a baby I was very fond of him. When I came back from a trip he used to say: 'Father, haven't you brought anything for me?' I used to be expecting him to say it, and if he didn't, somehow I felt disappointed. It was a strange thing. When he was six or seven he would say: 'Father, let's wrestle at Sumo,' and I would say: 'All right, let's,' and we would close. I am getting on in years, but against a tiny child like that, if I had thrown him he would have gone ten or twenty feet. But I used to play the part of putting out all my strength and then I would fall right over and he'd shout with joy: 'Father's lost, Father's lost!' There is a verse by the Zen master Gaun: 'I am a giant in power, but at a puff of wind I fall'– profound is the meaning.

When he was ten he was all the time asking for a bicycle; even at mealtimes he always came back to it. In the end this old abbot lost again and bought him an old second-hand one. Strange it is that even the ordinary human heart, which is no Buddha-heart, to help the children will go along with them like this. No one feels, when bringing up their tiny grandchildren: 'O ye dull deluded ones!' At that time, is it not a world different from the world of values?

Here there are no worlds of relative values such as the ordinary world and the sage's world, the defiled world and the pure world. For the liberation of all living beings, leaving all the worlds of relative value, having nothing in the heart, seeing the true form of all, this is the 'not defiled, not pure'. There is no dividing into pure and impure.

A SECOND ZEN READER

THE WORLD TRANSCENDING VALUES

In one of his sermons, Zen master Dogen speaks of realisation as knowing that the eyes are at each side with the nose straight down in the middle. No longer deceived by others, he returns with nothing in the hands, without one hair of Buddhism.

'Realising the eyes at the sides and the nose straight down, I was not deceived by others.' Though a hundred, a thousand people come to cheat him, this sort of life is one which is not taken in. With us it is not so; when they whisper behind my back: 'What nonsense the abbot is talking!' I get the disturbing thought: 'Am I?' But Dogen, who has realised the eyes on each side and the nose in the middle, is never deceived by them. The state of experience is expressed by the phrase 'returning empty-handed'. I came back from China without anything in my hands, without bringing one scroll of the scriptures or any other kind of holy learning. I have not one hair of Buddhism. Great Dogen says he has not one hair of Buddhism. From this returning empty-handed came the great Soto sect with its 14,000 temples.

In empty-handedness is there distinction of ordinary man and sage? Surely the life of Master Dogen was transcendence of values and seeing everything alike. To have a taste of the world of Emptiness we must make at least some effort to separate ourselves from the world of relative values. Though we may not have attained it, yet if in our passage amidst the illusions of attachment there has been a hint of awakening, we should just be making an effort to wish to transcend values. In this effort is spiritual training, and so it is that every movement of the hand, every step of the foot, is training. Our training should be towards transcendence. In the railway train in conversation with people I must make the effort to do it.

One time I found myself late at night at Fukui station. The train was going to a pilgrim centre and many pilgrims got on. On either side of me were old men and women. I was wearing simple clothes with just a round hat, and I suppose I didn't look to them like a priest. I asked whether they were pilgrims and if so where they were going, and they told me they were on the way to Minobu mountain at the suggestion of their families. I said that would be interesting for them, and one of them broke in: 'We're going to Minobu, where are you going, Grandad?'

At that moment, how is it if one is carrying anything in the heart? For an abbot to be addressed as Grandad! One would not be able to reply. It is here that is the spiritual training, to be called Grandad and from the bottom of the heart to be so. I said: 'Why, I'm off to Nagoya, you know,' and then we struck up a pleasant conversation.

We came to the junction at Maebara and while I was getting my things together the pilgrims had already got into the other train, except one old woman who got separated from the party and was lost in the subway tunnel. As I came past she recognised me and cried: 'Dad, which way is it?' Now from Grandad I had just become Dad. So I told her the way, and Dad and the old woman went along together.

Our training is in just such things. If an old man comes, then an old man, and if an old woman then an old woman. If a child then a child, and if a deluded man then to become the heart of a deluded man. In this sort of world there is no dividing into good and evil. To take good and evil as they are is the world of Emptiness of the Buddha. Not defiled and not pure, it transcends distinctions of ordinary man and sage, illusion and satori.

THE WORLD WITHOUT INCREASE OR LESSENING

If as the Sutra says it is neither increased nor lessened, then we may suppose that it must be an amount. In such case, is it large or small? But no. Long and short, square and round, these are the qualities of relative sise, but the world of Emptiness transcends the relational amounts.

So Zen master Dogen says: 'Turning in the fingers a vegetable stalk, he establishes the temple of the Lord of Dharma; in every grain of dust entering, he revolves the wheel of the Law.' In the monastery there is the Tenzo or one who is in charge of the food, and this is in the instructions for the Tenzo. Those in charge of the food, when they pick up the stalks in their fingers, must do it with the same firmness as establishing the temple of the Dharma-Lord, who is the Buddha. When the cook takes up the vegetable stem, it must be with the same power as building a mighty temple for the installation of the Buddha. Sweeping an almost invisible grain of dust, he must express the power by which the Buddha turned the wheel of the Law by his preaching. From the world of ultimate Emptiness, the world of quantity is transcended.

The spiritual training of Dogen is all Buddhism of action. Our Buddhism has to be manifest in every movement of the hand and every pace of the foot. Taking up the food must be with the firmness of establishing a mighty temple, lifting and lowering the chopsticks must be with the power which turns the wheel of the Law. Not in great matters alone is there to be the great manifestation – in the tiniest thing we must grasp the power which pervades the universe.

In the instructions to the kitchen Dogen says that everyday foods must be called by their elegant and respectful names, and in this too is to be manifested the power which turns the wheel and establishes the temple. Such elegant words may seem over-refined, but he directs that vulgar words must not be used and even a grain of rice must be spoken of with respect. The world of calculation and quantity is transcended and this is the world of real Emptiness.

Neither born nor dying, neither defiled nor pure, neither increased nor lessened: the triple transcendence has been taught to Shariputra, and then the Buddha says: 'Therefore in Emptiness there is neither form nor sensation, thinking, impulse nor consciousness.' This is the flavour of Emptiness. In our daily lives we have been leaving tracks of great evil but now there be not the least trace left by our steps. It seems to be rather negative, but this word 'nor' reveals the form of Suchness in which our steps leave no trace behind us.

6. THE EXPERIENCE OF EMPTINESS

*'So in Emptiness there is neither form nor sensation,
thinking, impulse nor consciousness; no eye, ear, nose,
tongue, body nor mind; no form, sound, smell, taste, touch
nor object of mind; no element of eye, nor any of the other
elements, including that of mind-consciousness.'*

MEDITATION WITH THE WHOLE BODY

This is the Emptiness of actual experience, the Emptiness of
entering faith and attaining realisation, not something just
thought about in the head. It is not a concept; the meaning
is Emptiness of actual experience. Master Dogen says in his
Bendowa classic: 'All are fully endowed with it, but while there
is no practice it is not manifest and while it is not realised
there is no attainment.' All have the potentiality but the fact
is that, unless it is practised and realised, it does not become
real. Now I set forth the essential points of the practice of
Zazen or sitting-in-meditation, strictly following the exposi-
tion of Dogen.

The monk must always begin Zazen by sitting in the correct
posture. After that he regulates the breath and controls the
mind. In the Mahayana there is also a method of observing
the breath, whether the breath is long or whether it is short,
and that is the Mahayana method of regulating the breath.

If we are going to realise the wisdom of ultimate Emptiness,
first we must perform Zazen, and for Zazen we must first sit
in the correct posture. In the Zazengi classic the method of

regulating the body is explained as control of movement, and the correct posture is a method for controlling bodily movement. Then there is control of breath and control of the mind follows naturally. The so-called fluctuations of the mind are controlled. The essentials of meditating with the whole body are: to control the body, to control the breath and then extend the control to the fluctuations of the mind.

In Hinayana they have meditations of counting the breaths and also meditations on impurity. Either they count their breaths or they meditate on the impurities of this our body. These too are ways, but the Mahayana method is simply to realise, at the time of meditation, that the breath is long or short. To put it more simply: according to the individual, the breath varies, long or short. Well, if long, let it be long, and if short, let it be short; one should just keep up meditation with the whole body on the going out and coming in of the breath. In his explanation, Dogen quotes the words of his own teacher, Master Nyojo. The master said: 'When the breath comes in it reaches the Tanden [just below the navel], but it does not come from any place so it is neither long nor short. The breath goes out from the Tanden but it does not go to any particular place so it is neither short nor long.' When the breath is inhaled it is drawn in down to the Tanden, a little below the navel. But it does not come from any place – the thing is just to feel it drawn down to the Tanden – and there is no point in inquiring where it came from. There is no need purposely to make it long or purposely to make it short. If long, let it be long, and if short, then short.

When the breath goes out, it leaves the Tanden, and has no definite place to which it goes. There is no point in working out where it ends up. Let each man leave his breath as it is, long or short, and just keep up with his whole body the meditation on the incoming or outgoing of the breath. There is no question here of trying to meditate with a Koan. It is devoting the whole body to meditation on the breath movement.

Dogen gives precise directions for when wrong and delusive thoughts arise during practice. In his Zazengi, of which there is a copy in his own hand at the Eiheiji temple, he quotes from the older Zazen classic (attributed to Hyakujo): 'When a thought arises, be awake to it; when you are awake to it, it will disappear. After a long time the associations are destroyed and spontaneously there is a coming to one. This is the secret of Zazen.'

If during the practice of meditation on the incoming and outgoing of the breath, various wrong thoughts and fancies arise, it is not that they are to be checked or suppressed. If we make to stop the movements of the mind, that attempt to stop them is itself a movement. There is no end to it. So it is not trying to stop the wrong thoughts, but being clearly conscious of them. 'Be awake' means to act consciously.

For example, I hear different sounds and the mind shifts towards them. Without trying to suppress this shifting of the mind, one should inquire: What is this wrong idea and fancy which has arisen? and so maintain clear consciousness in regard to it. What are all these things I hear? What is this thinking about them? In this way I am clearly conscious in regard to the disturbance of the mind. By doing this, in the end the wrong thoughts and fancies spontaneously vanish. 'After a long time...' when this meditation is continued not just one or two days but for years and years without a break, 'the associations are destroyed'. Of the two joined by association, one is subject and the other object; both of them disappear. The subject is the mind, and the going forth to experience is its operation. The object, which is the counterpart to the mind, is in Buddhist terminology called the 'field'.

To take an example: I hear a sound. The hearer is the subject, my mind. This is a pleasant sound, that is an unpleasant sound – the mind experiences like that. The object is the sound experienced. Similarly, whatever we see, the seer is the subject, the mind, and the seen, whether long or short or square or round or black or white, is the object. The word 'en' or association takes in the mind which goes to experience and the field which is the object experienced.

As we continue our meditation, finally the experiencer and experienced disappear. The disappearance of these two correlates is what he means by 'spontaneously there is a coming to one'. When it is said that meditation has gone into samadhi or has become one, it means a state when these two correlates become a unity.

LIVING WITHOUT LEAVING A TRACK

When the opposition of subject and object disappears, that is the condition of the real Emptiness. They have become one. Hitherto at each step in life a great imprint was left behind. While there are hearer and heard, at every sound arise the three passions of greed, anger and folly. While there are seer and seen, our mind sets them in opposition, and the different passions arise. While the two confront each other, while they have not become completely one, we are always leaving at each step a track which is the root of evil.

But for one who has actually realised Emptiness, both seer and seen, hearer and heard, disappear, and he can walk in life without his tread leaving any trace. To leave no trace is 'nothingness'. So often is mentioned this 'nothing, nothing', and we have to understand what it really means.

To laugh without leaving behind any trace of the laughter, to weep without leaving any trace of the tears, to rejoice without anything of that rejoicing remaining behind – this is a state of lightness, and to be able to live in it is the life of Emptiness, life with nothing at its heart. Then not one of the five skandha-aggregates leaves any trace, their forms are all the forms of Emptiness. In Emptiness there is neither form nor any of the others. (Under form are included speech and actions of the body.) Though speaking and doing, no trace remains of speech and action. The other four are mental functions, and of these mental functions also no trace is left.

The text continues: 'no eye, ear, nose, tongue, body nor mind; no form, sound, smell, taste, touch nor object of mind.' These twelve are called the 'entrances'. The first six are termed the six roots or organs; they are the six roots of subjectivity. Strictly speaking the five sense-organs are connected with awareness; the sixth is mind, which is mental functioning. Then over against the subject are the six 'fields' of form, sound, smell, taste, touch and mental objects.

The technical meaning of the word root is 'life-bearing'. In us is the sixfold subject, and therefrom arise the thoughts of right and wrong and good and bad and so on. Vis-à-vis the six roots are the six fields. The six roots are our subjectivity and the six fields are the objectivity; it is when there is a mingling, a confusion between them, that the delusive ideas and wrong thoughts arise. This mingling and mutual confusion are called the twelve 'entrances'.

Suppose I have only just heard of this teaching. Before that I was one who did not realise my delusive thoughts to be what they are. I was confounding subject and object, and so delusive ideas and wrong thoughts were appearing. With the clinging attachment to self, the delusive ideas were arising through this confusion, and they were painting a world of right and wrong and good and bad in which I was living in delusion.

Zen master Dogen speaks of it: 'Days and months, for a hundred years, I was enjoying only meanness of sound and form.' The hundred years is the wrong life up to the present. Sound and form here typify the whole six of the regions. Till now I was living just drawn by sound as I heard it, by form as I saw it. A long life indeed, pulled willy-nilly along as the impulses came. If the sound was unpleasant I was angry, and if pleasant then delighted – so I have been living just as the pulls came, in confusion of subject and object.

A hundred years of days and months I have been enjoying only meanness of sound and form. 'Yet in this state if I perform even one day of spiritual practice...' If I realise the character of these illusions and continue to meditate on it then though still pulled along, at each step I can experience the world of Emptiness and find the world of liberation of Kannon Bodhisattva, and know the feeling of holding nothing in the heart. How is it to be done? It is by the power of spiritual discipline, the discipline of Zazen.

What is this anger which rises, what is this complaining, what is this greed? In this way we directly confront the wrong thoughts and ideas which arise day and night. If on them we perform our spiritual discipline, we become able to have a little taste of the world of Emptiness. Emptiness is not to be a concept in our heads, a sort of contentless void. It is something to be realised in actual experience. To have nothing at the bottom of the heart is to experience Emptiness; then we see but it leaves no trace, hear and it leaves no trace. From the confusion of sixfold subject and object, we have been pulled along, but now our steps leave no track and we know the experience of being light. 'Nothingness' means lightness in this sense, the joy of leaving no track behind.

MAKING THE HEART EMPTY

In what follows I am taking the ear and hearing as representative of the whole set of six, and when it is said for instance that the opposition of hearing and hearer disappears, it must be understood to apply to the others also.

Now the sounds we make in the form of speech – there are two alternatives: either they issue from the state of Emptiness or they issue from the state of holding things. If we are not holding anything in the bottom of the heart and we can speak from the state of Emptiness, then in regard to those sounds there is neither hearer nor heard.

When I first came to my present temple I found I was getting a bad reputation as uncivil and unsociable. I tried to think what it might be, but I could not see that I was uncivil.

I took a lot of trouble over being civil. If an old lady came with a radish to offer to the temple, I used to say: 'It really is extraordinarily good of you to have brought such a fine radish and please accept my gratitude. And may I inquire after your health and that of your family?' And yet, the reputation remained. 'How awkward he is to get along with,' they used to say, 'not civil at all.' I gradually began to understand. It is quite inappropriate to say to an old woman with a cloth round her head: 'May I inquire after your health?' And when I was saying 'It is extraordinarily good of you to have brought such a fine radish', I had something at the back of my mind.

Well, I changed, and when I met an old lady on the way I did not say: 'Madam, may I inquire whither you are bound?' but instead: 'Hullo, Mum, where are you off to? Keeping well?' And gradually things changed and I had a good reputation for being very civil.

One may repeat elegant phrases a thousand times, but if there is something at the back of the mind there is the opposition of hearer and one who is heard. If there is nothing in the heart, and complete unity, then the simplest phrase doesn't have any opposition in it – there is just one. And words where there is neither hearer nor heard are the world of Emptiness.

The patriarch Dogen quotes a poem by his own teacher which he estimates as unique in spiritual illumination:

> The whole body like a mouth, hanging in emptiness,
> Not asking whether the breeze be from north or south, east or west;
> For all alike declaring the Prajna wisdom – Ti-ting-tung-liang, ti-ting-tung!

He saw a little bell hanging in a mountain temple, hanging in the emptiness. Hanging in emptiness means not to set oneself in some permanent position.

We often use the phrase 'to settle down'. People say 'Your Reverence' and one settles down in the Your Reverence and then replies. When they ask him something as Prime Minister, he first settles himself as Prime Minister. But with the Buddha's sermons, the whole body is a mouth, namely it is a unity, and so he speaks. He has no fixed form. Whereas with me, if I'm going along the road and someone asks: 'Your Reverence, may I inquire where you are going?' I say: 'Why, I am going to such-and-such a meeting . . .' I have been addressed as Your Reverence and my answer is extremely polite. But suppose someone shouts unexpectedly: 'Hey, Baldy! Where yer goin'?' Then what? I do not find a reply. If my head is shaved, it is for your sake ... what is this 'Baldy' to a Your Reverence? ... I am stuck in Your Reverence and cannot make a real reply.

When the whole body becomes a mouth – to speak negatively, Emptiness, and to speak affirmatively, Unity – without being fixed to anything, then if a word comes it is the form of the holy Buddha. The Buddha is one who puts himself in the condition of Tatha-gata, 'thus gone'. He never boasts of himself as Tatha-gata; the Buddha forgets Buddhahood and acts for the release of all beings. He who settles himself in Buddhahood is no Buddha. Buddha forgets Buddhahood and then teaches. Not asking whether the breeze be from north or south, east or west, it is all the same, he never goes against it and so he can speak.

When a beggar comes he can speak to the beggar, when a noble comes he can speak to the noble. However high an elder may come, he enters the feeling of an elder and speaks to him. He will never be reluctant, they are all absolute sameness. Whoever they are it is the same, there is no slightest bias, no reluctance; for the welfare of all he speaks of the wisdom of ultimate Emptiness, the wisdom of holding nothing in the heart.

Without this teaching there is no touching the hearts of the people. I am speaking of it, but I cannot attain it. Yet if one speaks from ultimate Emptiness, that man may weep but his tears have power to save all the people. He manifests the appearance of affectionate love and in that love is a power which saves all. And if he manifests the appearance of anger, in those very words of his there is a sublime power of salvation.

THE VOICE FILLING HEAVEN AND EARTH

Whether this instance will be understood or not I don't know, but it is something from a good many years ago, concerning Zen master Kitano Gempo. When he went to the inaugural ceremony of Joanji temple, some of us were in attendance on him. On arrival, a young monk brought tea for him. He had at one time been an acquaintance of the master, and so as he presented the tea he said in a familiar way: 'Welcome, master,' and just nodded his head in a half-bow. Zen master Kitano made no move to drink the tea: 'What is that head doing? To learn how to lower the head is the first thing in spiritual training; one who cannot perform the practice can never give spiritual help to others. When you lower your head, bring it right down and apply it to the mat. Why can't you make your bow with the whole heart?'

It is great teaching. When we have failed to do things with the whole heart, we must be profoundly grateful for a reprimand. One who has tasted even a little of the state of Emptiness – his teachings, his every word, are manifestations of the wisdom of ultimate Emptiness.

In the poem about the bell in the wind, the Ti-ting-tung-liang, ti-ting-tung is the sound of the bell. So an ancient said: 'His tongue covers the thousand universes, His words reach to Samadhi.' Unless the tongue is so great it hides the universe, he cannot really say anything at all. The point of view is that the holy teaching is limitless. The body has no limits, the voice has no limits. Life is limitless. It is in the Lotus Sutra. From the state of Emptiness, each man's body is a body pervading the universe, his voice is a voice filling the universe, his life is a life which is without limit.

The voice when there is no hearer or heard is the great voice which is pervading the innumerable universes. This is our own voice when there is no opposition of hearer and heard. It is limitless, but not in some abstract way; it is the condition in which subject and object cease to be.

Dogen quotes from Nagarjuna the story of one of the Buddha's ten great disciples, holy Maudgalyayana, who excelled all in psychic powers, and who once wished to measure the power of the voice of the Buddha. But the Buddha's voice was heard clearly by all the 84,000 to whom he preached. Nevertheless, the disciple felt that it must have some limit, so he projected himself through space by his psychic power, crossing countless thousands of millions of regions. He paused to rest on the shore of a place which faced a serene ocean. At this time the Buddha of that world was being served by a disciple with soup in a vessel which was called Adaptable. An insect flew to the lip of Adaptable and settled there, its head being like that of a man. All the disciples wondered what sort of an insect it could be, with its human head, but none of them could give it a name.

They took the bowl with the insect on it to the Buddha of that region and he said: 'This is no insect. Countless thousands of millions of regions away, a Buddha named Shakyamuni has appeared and is teaching many people. One of his disciples named Maudgalyayana wished to find the limit of his voice and by magic power he has come here; believing that the Buddha's voice will now be inaudible, he has settled on the edge of the bowl.'

The ocean was the soup in the bowl Adaptable. The Buddha admonished the insect-Maudgalyayana: 'You thought to calculate the limit of the Buddha's voice, relying on your magical powers, but you did not allow for the limit of those your powers. The voice of the Budddha fills the whole universe.'

So it is that there can be a power in our everyday speech which is not limited. When we can speak without anything in the heart, when from the bottom of the heart it is only unity, when there is neither hearer nor heard, then the words penetrate to the hearts of all. And when there is neither hearer nor heard, we can listen to that voice all day and there be no track left behind. In fact, when we can really throw ourselves into listening to anyone's voice, we shall do so without its leaving a trace. Seeing but without a trace of seeing, hearing but without a trace of hearing; when with the sixth sense-organ consciousness we think but without a trace of thinking, we can live unburdened and no track of sin behind us. May all experience it.

THE EIGHTEEN ELEMENTS

We have spoken of the five skandhas and the twelve entrances. Now there is another analysis – into eighteen 'distinctions'. As previously explained, there are six roots – eye, ear, nose, tongue, body and mind – and six fields – form, sound, smell, taste, touch and dharma-object – and six consciousnesses – eye-consciousness, ear-consciousness, nose-consciousness, tongue-consciousness, body-consciousness and mind-consciousness. It is the interaction of these three sets – roots, fields and consciousnesses – which manifests the world of illusion at every moment.

A full explanation is technical and may seem a bit complicated, but here it is: The twelve entrances were the six roots and the six fields. Now we can also take as subject the six roots and six consciousnesses, the object being just the six fields. We have in fact analysed the mind-root out into six consciousnesses, from eye-consciousness to mind-consciousness. At first it was the six roots which were the subject and the six fields the object, but in the classification into eighteen, the six roots and six consciousnesses as subject stand opposed to the six fields as object. And in the six consciousnesses, the eye-consciousness and the next four are functions of simple direct consciousness.

It is said that the eye sees shape and sees colour, the ear hears sounds. Now the simple direct consciousness of what is seen by the visual sense or what is heard by the auditory sense is a function of the mind, and these functionings are called the five consciousnesses of eye, ear, nose, tongue and body. The function of the sixth consciousness is to discriminate what has been simply taken in by the other five, discriminating into good and bad, painful and pleasant and so on.

The first five copiousnesses directly perceive things. Something is apprehended as white; now what is that which is simply apprehended as white? The function of the sixth consciousness is to consider and discriminate the whiteness.

So that besides the twelve entrances – six roots and six fields – there is this more detailed analysis of the mind into the six consciousnesses. When the Sutra says: 'In Emptiness there is neither form nor Vedana, Sanjna, Sanskara nor Vijnana,' it negates the five skandha-aggregates. Then 'no eye, ear, nose, tongue, body nor mind, neither form, sound, smell, taste, touch nor object of mind' negates the twelve entrances. Then 'no element of eye, nor any of the other elements including that of mindconsciousness' negates also the eighteen 'distinctions'.

Taken together, what we label skandhas, entrances, distinctions, are the form of our illusory clinging to self.

In whatever way the analysis may be made, whatever is on the basis of subject-object has no real existence or real nature. It is in order to show how on this no-reality arises our illusory clinging to self that the analyses are made. When everything has been analysed there is no definite self anywhere, but although there is none, a clinging attachment to self somehow arises, as if there were one. And on that, by the connection of subject and object, we are being impelled all the time by sounds which have no reality in them, by forms which have no reality in them, and thus pulled along we are committing sins in our wretched human life.

When in the midst of this life we gradually come to recognise what we are, then the grace of holy Kannon manifests and we have a taste of Emptiness without any burdens.

Living without carrying things means that, though we weep, the weeping leaves no trace, and when we laugh it leaves no trace of the laughter. This is the meaning of the continual 'No, no'. The ordinary man's delusion is in fact a deep-seated clinging to life. The desire just to live long whatever may happen is the illusory attachment to life. But in the midst of that very clinging is the world of release, and in fact, the deeper the clinging to life, the more clearly is release known. The stronger the passions show themselves to be, the deeper the experience of the Buddha salvation. The spirit of the Bodhisattva is to find salvation in living itself.

7. THE BODHISATTVA SPIRIT

*'No ignorance and no extinction of ignorance, nor any
of the rest including age-and-death and extinction of
age-and-death; no suffering, no origination, no stopping,
no path; no wisdom and no attainment.'*

THE HINAYANA IDEAL

Hitherto we have been speaking from the standpoint of the
ordinary man under illusion. Even in the midst of the illusions
it is possible to discover the world of Emptiness. It has been
said that even while we are being pulled along by life we can
experience that lightness of life when seeing leaves no trace
and hearing leaves no trace and there is absolutely nothing in
the heart. That experience is the joy of the wisdom of ultimate
Emptiness. Now we pass on to the attempt to experience the
true world of Emptiness in the twelve Causes and four Truths:
it is the attempt of those of the Hinayana path who are called
Shravakas and Pratyeka Buddhas.

Whereas the Mahayana Bodhisattva spirit would find the
true form in the ordinary man's delusions, the practice of
those of the Hinayana who are called Pratyeka Buddhas is
to annihilate completely all love and grasping and to negate
completely human life. Their ideal of Nirvana is utterly to
destroy the individuality. From love and grasping arise the
various illusions, and if those two are completely annihilated
and made void, there will not be any illusions.

The technical term for this annihilation of individuality is: extinction of existence and feeling. Body and mind are altogether negated, and this is said to be the Nirvana ideal. The true release from birth-and-death is (they say) to be born no more. Being born and dying is pain, and the destruction of existence and feeling altogether is their ideal state which they call Nirvana.

Then the text says: 'No suffering, no origination, no stopping, no path.' These terms belong to the Shravakas, who also following the Hinayana have as their final goal the annihilation of life. But the method of practice differs slightly.

The Pratyeka Buddhas go into the principle of twelve Causes in order to extinguish birth-and-death. Those called Shravakas are said to go into the principles of the four Truths in order to bring about the same objective. The twelve Causes are referred to in the phrases 'no ignorance and no extinction of ignorance, nor any of the rest including age-and-death and extinction of age-and-death'. The second set of phrases: 'no suffering, no origination, no stopping, no path', refers to the Shravakas who by practice of the four Truths aim likewise at extinction of life. What follows is a little technical but please bear with it.

I first propose to set out the Buddhist doctrines of delusion, karma-action and pain, and then to discuss the Hinayana view. The triad – delusion, karma-action and pain – is the Buddhist view of life in both Mahayana and Hinayana. Delusion means deluded grasping at something; it is sometimes called the passions. In Buddhism the delusion is the deep-seated conviction of an I where there is no I, in other words the delusion of hanging on to the I.

On this arise in the heart the forms of the passions, which thus are simply the mental functioning on the basis of deluded grasping. Though there is no self, the conviction that there is one leads to desire to satisfy the self by search which can never come to an end. Though something pleasant is encountered, the greed for more goes on without end. When something unpleasant is encountered, anger rises. Greed is first and anger is second. Third is folly and it is failure to understand the nature of things. One does not see the chain of cause and effect, that if one does good then there is good, and if evil, then evil. When we hear people grumbling all the time, we tend to think that they are just talking nonsense, but in fact their foolish talk is a sort of justification of themselves. It is the delusion of self-justification. It means that having done something wrong, we want somehow to make it out to have been right.

Suppose one gets up early while it is still dark, and on the way to the bathroom one stumbles against a water jar on the ground and breaks it. 'How clumsy of me!' and the wife replies: 'It wasn't your fault, I ought to have put it away.' There is no foolish complaining because each side is looking at its own fault.

But we don't do it like that, but instead attack the other party by saying: 'Who's the fool who left that here in the dark?' and the retort comes back: 'Who is it that goes blundering over it and then complains?' and the wrangle is on. All the time trying to make oneself out to be right is the sin of folly.

Well indeed if we could just sweep away all these poisons of delusion in the heart; but these our delusions cannot be ended just like that. They manifest themselves in every action of ours, and this action is what is called in Buddhism karma. Word or deed, our action is karma, and in it the movement of our mind infallibly reveals itself. He who outwardly inveighs against anger finds himself a murderer. The inner state is revealed in words and deeds, and such are called in Buddhism karma-actions.

Good or bad, there is the action, and I can never evade responsibility for it. With the action, an energy is implanted in me. The aggregate of the energies thus accumulated is also called karma, or karma-force, and it never becomes extinct until it has produced a result. At some time, it must bring about its result. Delusion and karma are like planted seeds, the fundamental causes of the results which we are bringing on ourselves. For instance, when a seed is planted, the seed itself is the direct cause, but by itself it will not sprout. There is the rain and the soil and so on, and only with these associated causes will it sprout. Then in the sowing which brings about the pains of life, the fundamental causes are delusion and karma-action.

THE PRATYEKA BUDDHIST VIEW

The fact that however much we try to act rightly we are unable to act absolutely rightly is the result of the karma of our past delusion and action. However we try to give up evil we cannot altogether give it up, and this is the effect of the karma-energy from our past. Our life of fifty or sixty years' suffering – and it must be called suffering – is just living all the time driven by karma through smiles and tears on the wheel of birth-and-death.

Delusion and karma-action, considered as the Causes of suffering in life, are again analysed into twelve, and the method of practice of the Pratyeka Buddhas is to perceive them in tranquillity, concentrated in the centre of the heart. The Pratyeka Buddhas meditate on the twelve channels through which delusion, karma-action and suffering are the causes of human life. Here is the list:

Ignorance, impulse (to live), consciousness, name-and-form, the six organs of sense including mind, contact, feeling (Vedana), desire, grasping, existence, birth, age-and-death. These are referred to in the Heart Sutra in the words: 'no ignorance and no extinction of ignorance, nor any of the rest including age-and-death and extinction of age-and-death'. Of the list of twelve, just the first and the last are expressly named, and the rest are included in the general phrase.

Ignorance means the passions. The heart which hangs on to self is the heart of passion. Delusion, action and suffering are all ignorance. *Impulse* to live is karma. These two are the Causes in the past, seeds which have been sown in previous births.

Delusion and karma created in former lives being the cause, our present life is the result, and it is classified into five: consciousness, name-and-form, the six sense-organs, contact, desire. *Consciousness* means the moment of the first throb of life in the mother's womb. It is the mental consciousness which is there at that first moment of life. As a matter of fact in Buddhism there is never mental consciousness without a body, but here the stress is laid on the mental side so the technical term is consciousness.

Then comes *name-and-form*. Name alone has no form and is a mental thing; form is the physical thing to which name is attached, and it means the body. The first is when consciousness settles in the first throb of life; the second period is gradual development of mind and body in the mother's womb; but as yet without the senses. Then is the next stage, of the *sense-organs*: eye, ear, nose, tongue, body-surface, and mind considered as the sixth.

Contact is one or two years after birth. The child stares and listens. There is just contact with what is before him, but he does not yet know about good and bad; it is just physical awareness.

The time of what is technically termed *feeling* is when having taken in what is before him he now begins to go over it all in his mind again and again. The condition of the mind where things are deeply gone over like this is technically called feeling. This is said to be the period from five or six up to fourteen years. These five (consciousness, name-and-form, the six organs, contact and feeling) are the fivefold Karmic effect in the present.

Now desire, grasping and existence. We come to the point when in our life which is a karmic effect, we come to produce passion and karmic action. Consciousness, name-and-form, sense-organs, contact and feeling are neither passions nor action. They create no sin. The child just touches the objects before him, and then up to fourteen he just takes them in. Up to feeling there is no sin whatever. But as the human being develops –according to one Sutra, from fourteen or fifteen up to seventeen or eighteen – the thoughts of desire and grasping begin to arise, thoughts of *desire* for sexual relations and accumulation of wealth and property. *Grasping*, the next in order, is when the thoughts of acquisition go deeper and deeper until the pursuit of them is incessant.

The manifestation in action of desire and grasping (which are thoughts of clinging to self) is what is technically called *existence*. It is another name for karmic action. As desire and grasping become strong they appear in our conduct and then the karmic energy, which will produce its results in the future, comes into existence. The time of creation in conduct, good and bad, of the karmic energy is technically called the stage of existence. Desire and grasping are passions; existence is karma. So that they form the pair – delusion and karma-action.

There were the five effects in the present: consciousness, name-and-form, sense-organs, contact and feeling, and now desire; grasping and existence are the three causes in the present, which lead to the two results in the future, namely birth and decay-and-death, or old-age-and-death.

The present spark of consciousness in the womb marks the future birth. The effect of name-and-form and the others is in fact age-and-death. Age-and-death is not in just the ordinary sense of something living which goes. It means to change round, it means mutability – for instance the way in which our destiny has brought about the changes of the five effects now.

So from the past to the present, and the present to the future; changing, delusion and action the causes, and age-and-death the effect, eternally we pass through the three worlds of past, present, future without ever reaching an end. Ignorance leads to impulse and impulse on through the others to age-and-death. So it is called a circle; because there is the passion called ignorance, there is action, and from karma-action comes about decay-and-death.

If the fundamental ignorance were cut off, there would be no action, good or bad; and if action good and bad were

Rinzai Zen monks engaged in walking meditation. This is a rapid walk around the meditation hall at intervals during meditation sitting. The walkers are expected to keep concentrated. (Courtesy of Shogenji Temple)

Waiting for admission. An applicant has to keep this posture of supplication for a couple of days (though he is occasionally driven away, which gives him a chance to stretch). (Courtesy of Shogenji Temple)

annihilated, delusion and karma-action would cease to exist. If delusion and karma-action ceased, there would be no more incurring of the suffering of life. If ignorance is annihilated impulse is annihilated, and so right up to age-and-death. This is the view of the Pratyeka Buddhas.

They mean it quite literally. First making passions void, they go on annihilating to become free from birth-and-death, and the annihilation of life is their ideal of Nirvana. The Nirvana of Hinayana is literally a void, nothingness. Their view is complacency at escaping from life. It is a selfishness which is satisfied with personal release from birth-and-death. So it is called the Buddhism of hermits and recluses in mountain and forest. Their Nirvana is annihilation of life.

The stick when bad posture indicates mind-wandering or sleep.
(Courtesy of Japan Broadcasting Corporation)

THE VIEW OF THE SHRAVAKAS

Those others called Shravakas see into the four Truths to obtain Nirvana of nothingness. These four Truths are said to be what is certain and without error. In the Sutra of the Last Teachings it is said: 'The moon may become hot and the sun cold, but the four Truths taught by the Buddha will never change.' Heaven and earth may be overturned but the principle of the four Truths will not be shaken. The four Truths stand on the doctrine of delusion, action and suffering already discussed. It comes down to this: Everything is delusion, action and pain. The present life is a result which has been incurred by delusion and action in past lives, and the doctrine of a power which brings about the result is the second Truth. The second Truth is that delusion and action in the past are, taken together, the fundamental cause of pain.

They speak of the path as the practice by which the fundamental causes have to be extinguished in order to extinguish suffering. To be free from birth-and-death, the causes (delusion and action) must be destroyed, and the appropriate practice is termed the Way, there being thirty-seven auxiliaries. Finally, by the way of practice which destroys delusion and action, there is attained realisation of Nirvana called extinction. Extinction is Nirvana. Extinction means that there is nothing. The extinction-Truth is realisation of a Nirvana in which life has altogether ceased to exist. So the practice of the Shravakas is to absorb the four Truths into the mind in the expectation of becoming free from life.

To sum up, both Pratyeka Buddhas and Shravakas think that our desire and grasping are things to be done away with. If they can be completely done away with, we become like empty snail-shells. Their Nirvana is in thinking that they have completely done away with the causes of life. In that they believe they have realisation.

This view, which would extinguish what is not to be extinguished, and which thinks it has been extinguished, is a shallow one; shallow indeed. Their Nirvana is an empty void, nothingness, and as such it has no meaning for life.

THE BODHISATTVA SPIRIT

The Bodhisattva spirit is different. In the midst of desire and grasping, which we cannot do away with however much we try, in the midst of our deluded thoughts and ideas, we are to try to discover the world of release. Day and night our desire and clinging make us alternate between joy and sorrow, laughter and tears. If there is something within reach I want to get it, but for all my efforts I cannot – in this state of desire and clutching let me discover the true world of release. It is through the existence of this very desire and grasping, or rather through the gradual coming to see that the character of this desire and grasping is the character of my self also, that I can come to discover release, and having discovered it to taste it and then to continue practice in faith. This is the spirit of the Bodhisattva.

The life of desire and clinging is: that all the time, though I think I will not get angry, anger arises. I think I will not say stupid things, yet they come out. It is possible for us to see every moment, in the deep passions which are the basis of life, our own true form. The deeper the desire and grasping, the more deeply can be experienced the absolutely unconditioned.

The spirit of the Bodhisattva is to find life at the heart of desire and grasping. Not for himself alone; he jumps into the bloodstained wheel of clinging to life in order to rescue all living beings.

Unlike the shallow Shravakas and Pratyeka Buddhas, the Bodhisattva seeks the true meaning of life. Contemplating in silence, this is the conviction I have reached. If I may be forgiven the personal reference, I may say that I find there is a meaning in the lowliest station.

Whether it is the true spirit of the Bodhisattva I know not, but I find that so long as there is security and health, and the environment is not *too* disturbed, I have attained peace. My present state is secure. There is no great disturbing passion. There do not seem to be karma-actions inspired by passion. And yet – the desire and clutching for life is a terrible thing. I catch a bit of a cold and go to bed. Someone says: 'Come now, you are in bed with a cold, how about thinking of the grace of the Buddha?' But my head is throbbing with pain – 'What do you mean? This is no time for thinking about the Buddha; my head hurts and I've nothing left to think with!' When we face the moment of death, with the convulsions and clutching for air, can we then sweep away the desire and hanging on to life?

It is said that a certain Zen priest at the moment of death gave the traditional cry of Zen illumination: 'Katsu!' But then another one is reported to have said: 'I don't want to die, I don't want to die!' Someone has well said on this: 'I suppose it is all right for a Zen priest to go on playing his part right to death, but for myself I find the "I don't want to die" has more human flavour about it.' One may be able to die with a 'katsu!' or one may not. But after all, in the 'I don't want to die, I don't want to die!', in the very thought realising that the character of the desire is the character of one's self also, in that last thought I verily believe there is the world of release.

CLINGING TO LIFE

Among the congregation of a country temple was a wife who contracted a very serious illness. She had to go to hospital in a town some distance away and her husband wrote me that his wife was very ill and wanted to see me. He asked me to visit her. So I made the trip and went in. She said: 'It's so kind of you to have come. I had thought I might never see you again, and I wanted to tell you something. I've been listening to your sermons in ordinary times and heard your teachings, and I believed that I really had faith in the world of release. But since I have been ill and come into hospital, my usual faith has been killed. I've got this illness which they don't seem to know what it is, and so all the more I ought to be remembering the Buddha with joy every hour and every minute. But I just can't seem to do it. Instead of thinking about the Buddha I find I can't help worrying about the house. I'm here in hospital but at home there's my husband and the three children. Even when I'm there it's hard enough to manage, but with me away in hospital what will they all do? I keep shutting my eyes and imagining it-the kimonos lying all over the place and the cups in the kitchen put away not washed, and the chopsticks left about and the whole place in a muddle. That's all I think about, when I ought to be thinking about the Buddha. But I never can... Your Reverence, what can I do?' She said this with great intensity.

I told her: 'It's very good that you have found this out. When things around are nice and safe and there's nothing wrong with them, people think they have acquired peace of the heart. But they haven't, you know. There's always the clinging to life

PART ONE ~ ON THE HEART SUTRA

and they can't give up this body. Now you see that you don't want to die till the children are grown up; you don't want to die until you feel everything has been settled.

'Our clinging to life is so strong. Now you have seen that this character of obstinately clinging to life is the character of your self also. Wanting to be happy and yet unable to be happy – that is what self is. It's very good that you have discovered it. It is through discovering that self is really just this desire and clinging, which can never be satisfied in spite of all efforts, that you come to know the world without conditions, the world of the Buddha's arms unconditionally open to all. With this you are released.'

With great joy she thanked me for these teachings.
My own small faith and experience is that the Bodhisattva spirit is not reducing life to nothingness and trying to escape completely into some Nirvana-world, but finding a meaning in this futile-seeming life as it is. And that is the real Nirvana.

By the Prajna Paramita ... to reach Nirvana. What is that state of Nirvana? It is not reducing life to a void. It is the feeling in life of an unburdened heart, of leaving no tracks behind, which is the real Nirvana. That is the attainment, that is the highest Nirvana.

When it is said 'there is no ignorance nor extinction of ignorance nor any of the rest including age-and-death', it means that from the standpoint of Emptiness there is no ignorance to be cut off, to be taken away. In Mahayana, if there is ignorance it is no obstacle. And so with the rest. If there is age-and-death, it is no obstacle. There is no extinction of ignorance and no extinction of age-and-death. The true nature of ignorance is Buddha-nature, the passions are the Bodhi, so it is not a question of extinction of ignorance. Birth-and-death is Nirvana, so it is not a question of extinction of birth-and-death. There is no suffering, cause of suffering, extinction of suffering, nor Way. There is no suffering, no cause to be reduced to nothingness. So there is no Way by which to put them away. Still less need there be some world of nothingness called Nirvana.

No wisdom, no attainment. In Hinayana the highest wisdom is realisation of the cutting off of delusion and karma-action, but there is no such wisdom and no realisation-attainment of some Nirvana-nothingness in which everything ceases to exist.

We have to experience the world of release at each step in life, and live lightly without leaving a track. There is still the present world of ignorance and age-and-death, the world of pain and the causes of pain, but they are no longer impediments. Rather it is just through them that we get the deep experience of being unburdened, and this is the secret of the repetition of the words 'no, no'.

8. THE EXPERIENCE OF NIRVANA

*'The Bodhisattva, since he is not gaining anything, by the
Prajna Paramita has his heart free from the net of hindrances, and with no hindrances in the heart there is no
fear. Far from all perverted dream thoughts, he has reached
ultimate Nirvana. By the Prajna Paramita all the Buddhas
of the three worlds have the utmost, right and perfect
enlightenment.'*

As explained before, it is only by the power of the wisdom of
ultimate Emptiness that we come to see that the inescapable
clinging to life is what we are. Through that power comes the
awakening to Emptiness.

Now the phrase 'he is not gaining anything'. If there
is no life which has to be reduced to nothingness then there
is no Nirvana which has to be gained; if there is nothing to
be thrown away, there is nothing to be grasped. Then what
to do? For baby Bodhisattvas like us, this is a question which
cannot be set aside even for a moment. There is no other way
than to discover the Bodhi in the passions themselves and
experience Nirvana in birth-and-death. The path which the
Bodhisattva must tread is one alone. There is no other path
except the power of wisdom of absolute self-negation.

Each step in birth-and-death is seen to be the true form of
the self. Passions are the Bodhi, birth-and-death is Nirvana.
By throwing away birth-and-death as it stands, however many
births and deaths we pass through they don't become Nirvana.
Ice is water, but if we simply throw away the ice as it is it still
remains ice and does not become water.

A SECOND ZEN READER

On the Bodhisattva path, when by wisdom he from the bottom of his heart knows what the self really is, he experiences the state of awakening. Now delusion, karma-action and suffering afflict no more. The karma-obstacles have disappeared. With the disappearance of the karma-obstacles the fear of birth-and-death in the six worlds also disappears.

'Far from all perverted dream thoughts.' It means he awakens from the dream of passions which arise from clinging to self. The bonds of karma are loosed, the fear of the worlds vanishes and he can really live as an awakened Bodhisattva, in the experience of Nirvana.

Now I speak only as a baby Bodhisattva. I am all the time being pulled by karma. But while being pulled along, I have discovered a real meaning in each step. May we all experience it! I am yet a child and there is no question that I am pulled; but I have a taste of the Bodhisattva world at each step. The state of being pulled is yet the state of freedom; there is no net of hindrances in the heart.

Another point is the disappearance of fear. Since I am alive, it cannot be that I never weep or laugh. But in that laughter – which is not a complete laughter – and in that grief-which is not total grief – I discover something of release, and then the laughter and the grief themselves are liberation.

The text speaks of awakening from confused dreams, Passions blaze up. But when the passion of greed appears I am to observe in its form the form of the self. In the form of passion I am to see the world of release, and so not be moved an inch by the passion. This is the experience of awakening and to some extent at least let us realise it.

When the text repeats its 'no, no' it does not imply nothingness. Tears and smiles, anger and desire, do arise; but the supreme Nirvana is verily to experience in those very things true Emptiness.

But we cannot rest only with this. The highest Nirvana means again to experience the world of exertion. To rest serene is not the height of Nirvana. I here digress from the text for a moment to explain the point.

THE HIGHEST LIFE

In Buddhism there are the Six Paths, which are worlds. And among them the world of humans alone is the noble one. These are the words of Master Dogen: 'A human body is hard to attain, the holy doctrine is rarely to be met with. Now, by our accumulated merit we have attained human form which is hard to attain, and met the holy doctrine which is hard to meet with – in all the worlds this is the best life, this must be the supreme life.' We must rejoice exceedingly at having been born in the world of men. For the Bodhisattva path of incalculable glory is only among men. Again he says: 'In the heavens taken up with pleasure, in the four lower worlds sunk in suffering, there is no opportunity for spiritual practice, and the aspiration of the heart is not fulfilled.' In the world of heaven they are obsessed with pleasure, and in the four lower worlds of hell, hungry ghosts, animals and demons they are sunk in pain. In these worlds the Buddha-heart does not manifest and spiritual training is very difficult. The reason in the case of the last four is that they are overwhelmed by their sufferings.

A SECOND ZEN READER

Instinctive grasping in the world of hungry ghosts, instinctive blazing up in hell, instinctive grumbling among the animals, instinctive resentment of others among the demons. These four are all merely driven by their karma and among them the Buddha-heart does not manifest. We at present are not to be slaves driven by karma. The Bodhisattva path is not for a slave instinctively clutching or instinctively flaring up.

I give a frivolous example. The monkeys which perform in the traditional monkey theatre, however well trained they are, at the slightest thing reveal their true instinctive nature. Once I saw a fine performance depicting the famous tragic scene (from the Forty-seven Ronin cycle) centring round the ceremonial suicide of the Lord Hangan. From one side came the monkey representing him, and as the singer chanted the words 'My retainer Yurannosuke not come yet?' the nobleman appeared to be expectant. From the other side now came Yurannosuke, and at the words of the narrator: 'He seems to be lost in thought,' somehow the monkey gave that very impression. Animals they might be, but they created feeling in one. Suddenly a spectator threw a bit of his fried potato between the Lord Hangan and his retainer Yurannosuke, paragon of loyalty. And Hangan forgot he was the Lord Hangan, and the loyal Yurannosuke forgot he was Yurannosuke, and they fought furiously over the potato. That was their world – at the smallest thing there they were driven by instinct after all.

Our lives are like this too. What sort of a home is it where the people instinctively clutch at things, storm over things, resent things all the time? It is the life of being impelled by karma, piling up sins. In such a world the reflection on self which they call the Buddha-heart will not manifest. There is never a hint of meditation on self. Parents wrangle and children squabble, old and young alike, and that's all.

The wisdom of ultimate Emptiness means to recognise what self is. It is not such a difficult thing. But those who have no power of wisdom are just pulled along, and are born in the four lower worlds, from which it is not easy again to return to this world of men. Because there all the time they are playing the role of suffering and fighting, so Master Dogen teaches us. What about the world of pleasure in heaven? This too is no case for congratulation, for they are entirely taken up with pleasure; all the time it is pleasure and pleasure. No inner reflection can come about. They have no chance to consider what the self is. The man who is singing drunkenly does not reflect on self. And these days there are many in such cases.

Once I was returning from Nagoya station to the temple when it began to pour and I took a taxi. The driver was a young man. With him as his assistant was a young girl who was not his wife. On the way he began talking: 'We're not young twice. However much you worry you can't help the way things are, so let's keep bright and cheerful.' And the girl said: 'That's right, we shouldn't bother about all these things; we'll keep bright and cheerful together.' This is dangerous. People these days often like to talk about keeping bright and cheerful, but that cheerfulness has its perils. So many think just to snatch enjoyment from each passing moment is all; they believe momentary pleasure is the meaning of life, that the thing is to live in some amusing or unusual way. They are people who think life is to satisfy the instincts. For such there is no self-reflection. The so-called heaven is a state in which the various human desires are satisfied, and since in such states there is no meditation on self, the Buddha-heart never stirs. And yet the Buddha-heart is not something which has to be sought afar. The turning of the thought in tranquillity on to the character of the self is the real Buddha-heart.

An abbot whom I knew was given charge of the education of the son of the local lord. He put him into a State school, thinking that the boy must get to understand a bit how others live. He used to tell me how the boy had no idea of doing the simplest things, nor any notion of the value of money, nor how to look after his own clothes. As a result for some time he found it difficult to get on at school.

From this we can see how when the desires are all satisfied there is no self-examination. It is not a particularly enviable condition. In the four lower worlds their role is to fight over the instinctive drives, whereas in the heaven the instinctive desires are satisfied. But satisfied or unsatisfied, they are simply worlds of instinct without self-reflection. For this reason we are taught that human life is of far greater nobility than those others.

THE EXPERIENCE OF CONTRADICTIONS

The Bodhisattva path is this: My I is not just the I which is being pulled along by karma. I struggle not to be drawn along by it. There is a faint experience of joy as I begin to realise the true character of that self which is still being pulled along in spite of all struggles.

When one is told: 'You're angry today,' he says: 'No I'm not!' In this world of contradictions, there is a joy in finding a certain flavour in those very contradictions. 'Why you're crying...' and even though the tears are falling, she says: 'No, I'm not crying.' There is a flavour in this self-control, and it is the spirit of a baby Bodhisattva. Perhaps I am biassed, but it seems to me that after over a thousand years of Buddhism there is in the Japanese people something of a like spirit.

When I have been talking from the pulpit for some time to the congregation seated on the floor, I sometimes say: 'Please sit at ease and not in the formal way; your legs must be cramped, but they reply 'Not at all' and keep their formal position however much it may really be so. No one will say: 'Yes they are.' When children fidget, it is better not to scold. If they have to sit still in the formal position and they begin to move their legs, instead of clumsily begging to scold them it is better to say: 'Oh dear, your legs must be cramped,' and then they say 'No they aren't' and straighten up. Self restraint of the natural inclinations is one of the best characteristics of the Japanese, and it is one element in the Bodhisattva path.

In the play Sendai Hagi, the nurse Masaoka sacrifices her own child to save the son of her feudal lord. Without a tear she addresses her dead baby: 'Oh, you have been loyal indeed; you be the spirit of loyalty for our land.' But then she breaks out: 'But it is a pitiful thing, that death should have the name of loyalty...' Holding back her tears, she is praising loyalty. There can be found something of that flavour in this life of contradictions. And I believe that the people in general do so.

When I am called to visit a household, the head of the house receives me in strict formal dress – 'is is so kind of Your Reverence to honour us with this visit and to accept our poor hospitality.' Inwardly he is thinking what a magnificent feast it is which he is providing. And I am cunningly hiding the thought that after my coming specially all this way it's the least they can do to show a bit of hospitality. Instead of this I say: 'Thank you so much for your really exceptional kindness.'

Japanese people don't express their feelings, and so some Westerners say that we are shy. It is true we do not show our feelings directly, but I don't think this is necessarily shyness. When a mother is going along with her little son, the people she meets say: 'What a dear little boy!' even if they think privately that he's a dirty little beast. On the contrary it is the mother who says: 'I'm afraid he is a dirty little beast!' while privately thinking what a treasure he is. Each side says exactly the opposite of what is thought.

But in recent times the Japanese people have begun to stop doing it, and that is a terrible thing and a very sad thing. For the Bodhisattva spirit is in controlling laughter and controlling tears, and finding release even when being pulled along unwillingly by karma.

There is a joy in seeing what is this I which all the time is trying to secure peace and yet which cannot attain it. The joy of seeing what it is that is trying and trying is the Bodhisattva spirit which continues its efforts through all failures, even for aeons of time. It is not what they call peace. Today failing, the next day failing, the Bodhisattva spirit is to continue unwearied efforts in the face of failure. Those who do not try are not seen to fail. To the Bodhisattva spirit, even failure has a sort of flavour. Insincere people do not know it; to the extent of his sincerity, a man knows it.

When I was young, I used to be sent to read the scriptures to any house where someone had just died. The teacher told me to look sympathetic and say: 'I deeply sympathise with you on the loss of your son,' or whoever it was. I always found this the hardest thing of all. I used to practise it to myself, but when it came to the point I stammered: 'Your son... your son's death... deeply...' and they didn't know whether I was condoling with them or angry at them. I tried hard but it never went properly.

I remember again at a service for the dead, when the Sutras are read in the open air, just behind me was the mother also reading. '*Na-mu-ka-ra-tan-no-to-ra-ya-ya*...' Why, there is someone just behind who has the Sutra. I mustn't make a mistake, I mustn't, and putting my whole soul into it I went on: '*To-ra-ya-ya-na-mu-o-ri-ya*...' and then dropped my voice so that her voice should also be heard. But just then the mother stopped also; all at once she stopped and there was nothing. Confused, I tried hard to pick up the thread but still nothing came. Certainly it is a fine thing to get everyone reading the Sutras together, but at my dropping my voice she had become nervous and dropped her voice too. When I think back to all those incidents of my youth, it seems that the harder I tried at things the worse they went.

Abbot Daisatsu of Kikoin temple at Nagoya was a great scholar. I remember the story of how once he went to read the Sutras at a ceremony but as it happened did not take the texts with him. Without any text he began to recite the Kannon Sutra. The mother of the family, who had the text, took it out and began to read with him. The Abbot was a man of very strong character, but it was a tricky situation. He did not have the text and behind him was the mother who had it. He had to recite it without mistake. As you will know, in the Kannon Sutra there are a good many places where the passages resemble each other. The Abbot found himself almost back at the beginning again; he was in a circle and could not get out of the Sutra. He began to perspire, and the mother, feeling sorry for him, said: 'Your Reverence, may we stop here?' The Abbot replied unbowed: 'If you wish we will stop here; as today's ceremony was so important, I have been reciting several times over the specially blessed portions of the Sutra.' At least, that's how the story about him goes.

From a man's efforts alone, there comes failure. Nevertheless, we can learn to appreciate the nobility of even fruitless efforts.

THE PARENT HEART

I had a boy student in my temple whom we had brought up from childhood. He had a peculiar nervousness which made him unable to stand out in front of people and speak properly. There is a ceremony at which one who wishes to take a particular rank has to answer questions from a good number of questioners. Along with many other youngsters, this boy was to take the role of asking some of these questions. I say that questions are asked, but in fact the whole thing is rehearsed; questions and answers both are fixed. You say this, then he says that, and now you say this, and so on. We wrote it all down for him on a sheet of paper and told him he must learn it by heart, that he absolutely must know it by heart for the day.

When the time came he went along with the party to the ceremony. All the others did well, and slowly it came round to his turn. His heart was like a big drum in his chest. When it came to he was as if in a dream, hardly conscious of himself at all. All passed off well almost to the end, when he had to say the Chinese syllables *Chin-Cho*, which means literally 'precious and venerable', but which is simply the ritual formula used on these occasions to indicate that the answers have been correct. He got these syllables turned round in his head so that they became *Cho-Chin*, which is the ordinary colloquial Japanese word for a paper lantern. Till then he had been perfect, but when it came to the end he could remember only that there was some short phrase he had to say. He hesitated and then suddenly thought he remembered it and *cried* out: The spectators could hardly contain their laughter; he alone did not realise what had happened.

After the ceremony the youngsters were coming back together and some of the spectators said to him: 'Why, you're the lantern boy!' and he found out what he had done. I had not been at the ceremony, but the senior boy came and told me that one of them had made a terrible blunder. Then the boy came in, very downcast, and I said: 'Did something happen?' 'Nothing happened.' I asked again: 'Surely something happened, didn't it?' and he repeated in a tearful voice: 'No, nothing.' I could not bear to pursue it – 'Well, if nothing happened, good; have your meal and go to bed.' 'I don't want to have anything.' He was about to break down, so I said: 'Then just go to bed,' and he made his bow and went.

The worry was left to me. This boy who was so gentle he would not harm an insect, he had done his best, had been overcome and now had gone to bed. I stole round to see how he was. He was like a baby asleep, everything forgotten, like a sleeping Buddha. I was held by that face. He had done his very best and then failed, and of all the people who knew what had happened, could there not be just one who did not laugh, who could sympathise? As I watched his sleeping form I had a strange feeling: though all the world laughs at you, there is one here who will never laugh at you.

This is the relation of pupil and teacher. And for our whole life there is One who does not laugh, who will weep with us without any reservations, a power which will receive us unconditionally, in all our struggles and failures. The Bodhisattva spirit gives meaning to every step in our lives, and even I have had a faint glimpse of it.

Look at the text once again. The heart is to be free from the net of hindrances. If we try to find the meaning when we are pulled by karma, soon we are no longer pulled by karma. We are free. When in each step of life we can find meaning, there is no more fear of the six worlds. In the midst of the flaring up of the passions, the world of release appears, and we can live a life which is not of the nature of passion.

The Bodhisattva drops the self by the power of the wisdom of ultimate Emptiness. Knowing the true nature of his self, he is freed from the character of delusion, karma and suffering.

It is going on with this our human life of frustration that is the form of the supreme Nirvana. It is the Nirvana of exertion; rest, even if attained, would not be the supreme Nirvana. Passing on and on without rest, experiencing Nirvana at each step – that is the true Nirvana.

'By the Prajna Paramita all the Buddhas of the three worlds have the utmost, right and perfect enlightenment.' The three worlds are past, present and future, and by the power of wisdom of ultimate Emptiness they attain perfection. The original phrase, which is almost untranslatable, is here rendered utmost right and perfect enlightenment. It means realising an experience which is unequalled, which is truth, which has no flaw.

Experience of the peerless and all-pervading is what is called wisdom or awakening. When the term 'true path' is used, it indicates the principle which is itself experience. So that sometimes the translation refers to the state of the experiencer, sometimes to the truth which is experienced, sometimes just to experiencing. It is called Sameness and universality; the Buddha-experience of the true form of everything is not something which here he experiences and there he does not. The meaning is that he experiences the true form of all beings and things.

The Buddhist doctrine is to see the Suchness of things. To come to see the true form of all is satori or Buddha-experience, and it is the same everywhere. What is the true form of Suchness? It is that the true form is formless, is no form. The form of the Buddha-experience is that all things are formless. In other words it is the knowledge of ultimate Emptiness. The Buddha's forgetting of the Buddha-form is the true state of no-form.

Since the Buddha is formless, there is no definite form in his heart, and so the Buddha becomes the heart of all. Master Dogen says: 'The Buddha is transforming himself in the three thousand worlds and never withdraws.' in all the spheres he manifests his form, he brings reconciliation to the tortured hearts of all and never withdraws from them. In truth the Buddha is not something at rest.

9. THE POWER OF PRAJNA

'Know then that the Prajna Paramita is the great spiritual mantra, the great radiant mantra, the supreme mantra, the peerless mantra, which removes all suffering, the true, the unfailing. The mantra of the Prajna Paramita is taught and it is taught thus: Gone, gone, gone beyond, altogether beyond; Awakening, fulfilled!!' (Gate, gate, paragate, parasangate, bodhi, svaha!)

This section we shall take in one. What is the wonderful power of the Prajna wisdom? It is the great spiritual mantra, the radiant, uttermost, the peerless mantra. Mantra is a Sanskrit word, which is usually translated 'spell'. In a spell there is the feeling of something over and above the words, and so it is that the term was used for the words of the Buddha which have inexhaustible depths of meaning in them. In each word of Buddha there is a depth of meaning, and hence they felt them to be untranslatable. It was thus natural that the mantras, or dharani as they are sometimes called, were never translated in transmission, but handed on in their original form.

The power of the Prajna wisdom is the great divine mantra; a profound and wonderful utterance of the Buddha. Then it is the great bright mantra, like a bright mirror without a trace of mist. It is the peerless mantra: sublime are the words of the Buddha. It is the mantra without an equal, peerless and transcendent.

Now we return to the first phrase, the great spiritual mantra. Spiritual powers are spoken of as miracle-working; to perform some extraordinary feat is commonly regarded as a manifestation of spiritual power. But surely it is not. To act from the wisdom of ultimate Emptiness, namely to act with the heart empty – this is all spiritual power and it is not what is called miracle.

In the Shobogenzo classic the teacher says: 'The one of right wisdom is a Buddha, a patriarch; he is always manifesting it. Working with cloth or pail, presenting tea or taking tea, it is a spiritual manifestation, a divine manifestation... What is called the great mantra is human affairs. Human affairs being the great mantra, the mantra is no other than manifestation in human affairs... Human actions of ordinary life are burning incense and reverent worship. The spiritual power of the mantra means to meet a man of right wisdom and serve him faithfully; it is offering tea and taking tea. These are the form of spiritual manifestation and there is no special miracle beyond that.

One thinks of the power of a mantra as something remote, but it is not so. The true spiritual power is in offering a cup of tea to the teacher. To serve with one's whole heart in the wisdom of ultimate Emptiness is the real miracle-working. The mantra is human affairs, and that human action is burning incense and reverent worship. Morning and evening to serve a teacher in reverence is a form of the mantra.

During the lifetime of Master Dogen, his successor Ko-un served him constantly; and every night and morning he used to make a salutation and inquire after his health. In the morning he would ask him: Master, how are you? and in the evening when the teacher retired he would prostrate himself and ask: Master, is all well? After the death of the teacher, he used to bow before the wooden image of his teacher and ask the same questions every day.

In this way in the ordinary things of our life we must use the spiritual power of the wisdom of ultimate Emptiness. So it is that the Prajna Paramita is the great mantra; it has the power of the great mantra. When we can pay reverence from the bottom of the heart, in that there will be a great spiritual power.

REALITY

Now the great radiant mantra. Without a speck of dust, bright like a mirror, the state of ultimate Emptiness reflects everything. A mirror leaves nothing unreflected. If a beggar comes it reflects a beggar, if a nobleman, then the noble. Whatever the form it reflects it, and this accommodation to any form is what is termed the bright mirror.

Long ago Zen master Seppo asked: 'What if you suddenly come upon a mirror?' To which his disciple Gensha replied: 'Into a hundred fragments!' Smash it to pieces was his reply. For while the heart is caught by something called a bright mirror; it is no real mirror, no mirror at all.

It happened a little time ago that a cabinet minister resigned, and he spoke of himself in the Chinese phrase: 'Bright mirror, still water.' Perhaps you will remember the incident. The meaning was that his heart was unmoved, that he felt like a mirror without a trace of clouding. It was like stilled water without a fleck on it, with no disturbance. That was what he seemed to be saying, but if all he meant was the bright mirror of stilled water, we may feel there was yet something lacking.

Isn't there something yet lacking in a man when he says he is a bright mirror in still water? If that is the sort of bright mirror and still water, then – into a hundred fragments! Until it is smashed up altogether it is no real bright mirror. This point may be a little difficult to appreciate. When it is done, each fragment must itself be a mirror. The tiniest sliver must be a mirror. In truth our bright mirrors have to become a hundred fragments.

What is this smashing? A master of our line warns us that the bright mirror is not water stopping still, but water breaking into thousands of drops and flowing on, adapting to any form that comes. Such is the bright mirror. To rescue one who has fallen into the mud, the Bodhisattva goes and himself becomes muddied. To save a drowning man he leaps into the water and rescues him by himself becoming wet. This is the breaking of the mirror into fragments.

For the sake of the people, the brilliant mirror of the wisdom of ultimate Emptiness is broken up into their hearts and comes to reflect everything there. It is not simply resting satisfied with being oneself a mirror. This is a point of profound significance.

Than such action there is no higher power, to it there is nothing comparable, and so it is peerless and unequalled. It sweeps away all suffering, suffering of any living being and under any circumstances. Here let us consider the pain of life and death as the type of all other pain. The Prajna Paramita is the power which releases from the suffering of the round of birth-and-death. The holy words of the Buddha never prove false, so say the Lotus Sutra and the Diamond Sutra. The Buddha's words are not like our talk, of which it hardly matters whether it is said or left unsaid, which is just to pass the time. He is not expressing, like us, some attitude which is fundamentally pointless. Nor is he speaking of abstractions. His every phrase, every word, has a sublime power to release beings from all sufferings, to free from life and death.

Now Master Dogen tells us: 'Know that merely understanding oneself to be Buddha is not knowing the Buddha way.' A mere comprehension of the proposition that all are Buddhas, of the truth that one is oneself Buddha, to say 'I understand it,' is not the same as knowing the Buddha way. Simply to have that understanding of the truth is not to be released from birth-and-death. When they speak of the words of the Buddha having the power to release, it does not mean just by an intellectual understanding. The true words of the Buddha are those which turn all beings from illusion and pain by enlightenment in them. It is not a question of intellect, it is not a question of saying 'I understand'. Buddhism does not say to the intellect: 'You are Buddhas – have you understood it?' The true words have to be powerful to release from all sufferings, and those alone are the truth-bearing words of the Buddhas and patriarchs.

THE STORY OF SOKKO KONIN

Here is an instance from the old records of Zen. A monk named Sokko enrolled as a pupil under the famous Master Hogen, but for a long time he never seemed to want to hear about Buddhism and never asked the master any questions about it. Then the teacher said to him:

'You have been my disciple for three years now, but you have never inquired of me about Buddhism.' In other words: Why is it that you ask nothing?

The disciple replied: 'Before I was with Master Seiho and I heard the doctrine and attained peace and bliss.' He declares that under Seiho he obtained satisfaction, that he attained realisation.

Then the teacher said: 'Through what words did you get what you sought?' He inquires what was the phrase which brought peace to him. Then Sokko related the passage of question and answer with his former teacher:

'I faced Seiho and asked him: "How is it, the self of this disciple?" He told me: "The lampboy is looking for a light."'

Master Hogen said: 'It is a fine phrase. But probably you have not understood it.' The words are well, but it is likely that you have not grasped them.

So Sokko explained how he understood it: 'The lampboy is in charge of the lights. Taking the light to go to look for a light is like my taking the self to look for the self' This is belief in the Buddha, and conviction that the Buddha is the true nature of the disciple.

'I knew it! You have not understood. If that were Buddhism it would never have lasted till now.' At first he said only that his disciple had probably misunderstood, but after the explanation it was clear that he did not know.

Sokko, it is related, was very upset and got up at once. His heart agitated, he muttered: 'What am I doing under such a fool?' and left.

After going some way, however, the thought came to him that Abbot Hogen was said to be one of the wisest of men, and spiritual director of five hundred disciples. If such a man declares there is a mistake, there must be something in it. And so he went back to the teacher.

'In repentance and reverence I ask... I have been wrong. I bow and ask pardon.' Then addressing the teacher, he asked: 'How is it, the self of this disciple?'

Now the Master Hogen replied: 'The lampboy is looking for a light.'

At these words, we are told, Sokko had the Buddhist enlightenment. He had the great satori. How are we to understand it? This is my own humble view:

> The first time the phrase was uttered, by Sokko, it was in the sphere of empty concepts; the Buddha was an intellectual Buddha, something thought in the head. The self is the Buddha – it was all no more than drawing a picture Buddha in thought. It called forth the response 'your Buddha is no true Buddha', which upset and enraged him. But after reflection he realised that the utterance of such an enlightened teacher must have a purpose, must have a deep significance, and so he went back and asked pardon.

Asking pardon has a very great meaning. It means a state of self-merging. 'Please forgive me' means merging what is called self altogether in the spirituality of the teacher, and when the self thus is naughted, in that very self-submerging is verily release, is awakening. He sank his self into the heart of the teacher named Hogen, and that was his awakening.

And then just one sentence, a single sentence of the teacher, had the power to change the bones and substitute a new core of life, the power to dispel illusion and open up satori, which transcends life and death. It is not teaching empty concepts. Not one word of the Buddha, not one word of the patriarch, ever fails.

When Shakyamuni reached the end of the Way, he first thought of the five ascetics who had served him, and went to the place where they had separated from him. They had resolved that if he returned they would not acknowledge him. But when he came from afar off, as he approached he said 'Good, good', and unconsciously they rose and saluted him. Their hair fell off of itself and the Buddhist scarf was round their bodies. It was a symbol that they had become his disciples and had gone beyond birth-and-death. When he spoke, without thinking they rose and saluted him. Their hair and beards fell off and instead the scarf appeared round their shoulders – it meant that they had attained realisation from that one phrase of the Buddha. Similarly the words of the Prajna Paramita are unfailing to give release to all.

So it is that there are infinite depths of meaning in the Prajna Paramita mantra. Of the great Prajna Paramita Sutra in six hundred books the Heart Sutra is the kernel, and of that kernel the phrase of the mantra is the kernel. It is in the original Sanskrit: Gate, gate, paragate, parasangate, bodhi, svaha! The traditional translation runs: Gone, gone, gone beyond, altogether beyond; Awakening, fulfilled!

Now I add a last word on this mantra of the Bodhisattva path. The mantra refers to the Bodhisattva path of Mahayana Buddhism. The word Bodhisattva may be split up as follows: Bodhi means awakening and sattva means a living being. The Bodhisattva is one whose sublime aim it is himself to awaken and to awaken the others. It has been said that he first

A SECOND ZEN READER

himself awakens and then awakens others, but in the view of the patriarch Dogen the Bodhisattva is one who undertakes that: all living beings shall cross beyond before he himself does so. Before fully awakening himself he will see that all others are awakened; the true Bodhisattva spirit is to leave himself where he is and undertake that all others shall first cross to the far shore.

'What if this foolish I do not become a Buddha?
Let me only be one engaged in taking others across.'

Let me not become a Buddha but let others become Buddhas first. The Buddha-heart is this: to labour ceaselessly with body, speech and mind to cause the Buddha-heart to arise in others and draw them to the Buddha-path. He spares himself not a moment's rest but breaks his bones in labouring to draw others along the Buddha way.

The futile attempt to gratify worldly desires has no value for living beings. To seek to fulfil worldly desires is not the Bodhisattva spirit, which is an uninterrupted exertion for the sake of bringing others along the Buddha-way.

Consider the words of the mantra. 'Gone, gone.' It is repeated, and it means crossing for oneself and crossing for others. And the view of the patriarch is that the others should cross first. Cross to where? To Nirvana, to the far shore. From this bank of the illusion of birth-and-death to the world of Nirvana which leaves no karmic track, to the sublime state of Nirvana, is the crossing for me and for others. 'Altogether beyond' means that all living beings are to cross, and the awakening is complete.

Here is the fulfilment of the Bodhisattva path of self-awakening and awakening others. And the view of Master Dogen is that the Bodhisattva Kannon still does not become Buddha, that the Bodhisattva Jizo for aeons in the future will not become Buddha. Before becoming Buddha, they will release all living beings.

There are people who say that the ideal of Buddhism is to live together and prosper together, and this principle will manifest real peace. But I believe this idea is a deplorable mistake. Buddhism is not living and prospering together, it is offering up one's whole body and mind for the sake of all living beings. That is the real Bodhisattva spirit. Mutual prosperity would mean that if there are ten things, then we divide them equally between us. But the question is, whether equal division of the spoil will in fact lead to peace in society.

Take a trivial example: I am asked out somewhere. In front of me are placed three of those delicious cakes of which I am so fond, and before my neighbour the same. As we each have three, there should be no cause for discontent. But it doesn't work out like that. When I look carefully at his cakes, they seem to be bigger than mine. We have both got three but his are bigger, and so it is that, even though there is equality in number, we need not expect to have a world of living together in mutual prosperity.

If we turn to great matters, say international relations, isn't it just as unreasonable to expect mutual satisfaction on the basis of numbers? You build five battleships and I will build five battleships. But it is impossible that peace should be attained just by equality of numbers. The principle of live and let live is based on sticking attachment to self and soon leads to a struggle. A world of temporary 'mutual prosperity' is built up on what they think is self, that's all.

Buddhism is not mere words, but whole-hearted sacrifice of body and mind for the sake of all. Though I do not become a Buddha, may I be of service to all beings in becoming Buddhas. It is when we can have this spirit in all our dealings that peace will be manifested.

Finally, for myself, let me live among the humble, let me labour at a thankless task, let me discover a real meaning in the circumstances in which I find myself. The whole of the Bodhisattva spirit is in those ultimate words of the mantra. The way of Buddhism is in the traditional prayer: May these merits reach all, and we and they together attain the end of the Buddha way. So with this ancient prayer that the merits of our study may be for the benefit of all, I close my discourse.

May the merits of our study reach all, and we and they together attain the end of the Buddha way.

Part Two

Yasenkanna

**An Autobiographical Narrative
by Zen Master Hakuin**

Illumined vision

1. INTRODUCTORY NOTE
by the translator

Hakuin (1685–1768) was the greatest light of Rinzai Zen in Japan. He universalised it and brought its flavour into the lives of ordinary people, and all the present lines of transmission run through him. The pattern of his spiritual life is thus of great importance in understanding Rinzai Zen. Yasenkanna (which can mean literally 'idle in a boat at night') is an account of a spiritual crisis and its solution, and a most illuminating Zen text. This and several other important works of Hakuin are in Japanese, accessible to the general public, whereas most Zen works of the time were in Chinese.

Hakuin left his home when he was fifteen in order to take up a religious life. At the time he had a great fear of the Buddhist hells. He studied the Lotus Sutra, the most important one for Japanese Buddhism, and his doubts crystallised round the Sutra, and also round the tragic death of a Chinese Zen master named Ganto. This master remained in his temple when others had fled before a gang of brigands; one of them ran a spear through him. Ganto's expression did not change, but he gave a great cry as he died, which was heard for miles. Hakuin was thrown into depression by meditating on the event; if even Ganto, the spiritual genius of his age, could not save himself from death at the hands of the brigand, how could an ordinary seeker like Hakuin hope to escape from hell? (The Dentoroku Zen history says that the teacher Ganto had always told his disciples: 'When I go, I shall go with a great shout' – a fact which may or may not have been noticed by Hakuin.)

He considered giving up Zen and devoting himself to poetry. It chanced one day that he saw the books of a temple library being brought out into the sun for the annual airing, which is the custom in Japan. He closed his eyes and walked towards the piled-up books, extending two fingers so that he should pick up just one. When he examined it he found he was holding a Zen book, and opening it at random he came on a passage relating how Abbot Jimyo, sitting long hours in meditation when the rest were all asleep, was invaded by the demon of sleep. The Abbot drove a gimlet into his thigh in order to keep awake. Hakuin found new inspiration in this revelation, and practised meditation-sitting assiduously. After a very hard life for some four years he was at the Eiganji temple, meditating at night on the Koan 'Mu' and in the day listening to the teacher's sermons on human and divine vision. When the course of lectures ended, Hakuin went quite alone to meditate day and night. After some days he passed into a state beyond thought and concept. Hakuin's writings repeatedly refer to this kind of experience; he compares it to being inside a diamond or a jar of lapis-lazuli, or sitting frozen to death in a field of ice. On the evening of the tenth day, the distant sound of a temple bell seemed to reverberate in his ears like the rushing of a flood, and the trance was broken. He had a flash of realisation, and found that he himself was Ganto, with not a hair-tip harmed passing through the three worlds. He shouted: 'Why, the world is not something to be avoided, nor is Nirvana something to be sought after!' This realisation he presented to the Abbot and some fellow disciples but they did not give unqualified assent to it. He however burned with absolute conviction, and thought to himself that surely for centuries no one had known such a joy as was his. He was then twenty-four. In his autobiographical writings, Hakuin warns Zen students with peculiar earnestness against this pride of assurance.

A disciple of the teacher Shoju recommended him to seek in that quarter, and he came under the hammer of a master who utterly smashed his self-satisfaction. After three years of harsh treatment, trying to grasp the 'Mu' and later another Koan, he one day passed into a state of meditation while standing in the street. An old woman struck him on the head with a broom, and as his trance broke he again had the great joy. His Koan was clear to him. Rushing home, he was received by the teacher with the words: 'You are through.' He had a dream in which his mother, to whom he had been devoted, told him that as a result of his spiritual merits she had attained a Buddhist paradise.

Hakuin classes this as a great satori. Soon afterwards he left to attend on a former teacher who had fallen ill. Shoju (who died afterwards and whom he never saw again) warned him not to be satisfied with a small thing but to perform the 'practice after Satori'. He also told him to try to make one or two good Zen students, and not to hope for more.

Though the realisation is accounted a great satori, and approved by the teacher, Hakuin later found that he still had some doubts about the Lotus Sutra, and that he could not disentangle the 'Five Ranks' (Koans) of Tozan. Tozan was one of the founders of the Soto sect in China; the Five Ranks are not so much favoured in the Japanese Soto sect because Dogen believed that they tend to lead to mere dialectics, but the Rinzai take them as the basis for high Koans. Hakuin studied them under a senior disciple of Shoju.

There followed another great crisis, which is the subject-matter of Yasenkanna.

When that was over, Hakuin for several years practised meditation in isolation, under conditions of extreme austerity, as his practice after satori. He was now full of extraordinary energy of body and mind. He was studying the Sutras, and the phrase is quoted: 'the ancient teachings illumine the heart, and the heart illumines the ancient teachings'. Hakuin records that several times he heard a music in the sky which continued until he recognised it as in his own mind, when it abruptly ceased. Another time he found himself overwhelmed by fear, which he finally managed to dissipate through the meditation: 'By what is fear experienced?'

He became a teacher at the tumbledown temple of Shoinji, with only a single disciple. Slowly others were attracted to him. In his forty-first year he was undertaking a meditation retreat in a private room behind the temple, reading the Lotus scripture by day and contemplating all night. He had another dream about his mother. This time he dreamt that she had given him a magnificent purple robe. The sleeves were heavy, and in them he found two mirrors, the right-hand one flawless and brilliant, but the other, in the left sleeve, dull like the bottom of a saucepan. As he took this second one in his hand, it suddenly blazed with light, outshining the first a million times. 'After this,' relates Hakuin, 'looking at the things of the world was like looking at my own face, and for the first time I understood how it is the Buddha-eye that sees the Buddha-nature.'

The next year he was sitting at night reading the Lotus Sutra when there came the sound of a cricket chirping. Suddenly he found he had penetrated into the uttermost depths of the

Sutra. The meaning of the ordinary daily life of his teacher Shoju was revealed, and he saw he had been mistaken over his great satori realisations. This time there was no great reaction in the body-mind instrument.

In the biographical writings summarised above, we see that Hakuin passed through several spiritual crises, some of them Koan riddles given formally by a teacher and others personal to him. More than once he had an apparently conclusive satori but found himself mistaken. The final problem turned on doubts about the Lotus scripture, and also perhaps about the daily life of his old teacher Shoju.

Hakuin's disciple Torei, in his biography of the teacher, divides the life so far into three sections: first, up to the great satori which centred on Master Ganto, and which took place when Hakuin was twenty-four; second, from twenty-four to twenty-eight, the training under Shoju which ended in a satori resolving the Koan given by Shoju; third, from twenty-eight to forty-two. The third period begins with the events narrated in Yasenkanna, and includes several great satoris, at least one of them connected with the 'Five Ranks'. It ends with satori-realisation of the profoundest meaning of the Lotus scripture. Everything up to this point is classified by Torei as activity of the nature of Cause; only after this begins the activity of the nature of Effect, continuing till the death of the master at the age of eighty-four.

Yasenkanna is the history of a Zen crisis written from within, so to say. The Zen illness there described arises from excitement and pride in a satori which is in fact only partial, coupled with the struggle involved in breaking down the conceit of self. The cure consists of psycho-physical exercises called collectively Nai-kan (inner contemplation, literally inward-looking), which Hakuin recommends to his pupils along with their Zen-kan (Zen contemplation) or Ri-kan (truth-contemplation), as two wheels of a chariot or two wings of a bird. In a number of his works he emphasises the Naikan practices and they are an important element in his thought.

There are problems connected with the chronology of Yasenkanna which need not distract the reader primarily interested in Zen. The existence of Master Hakuyu is established, and specimens of his calligraphy exist. His method of Naikan is mentioned by the famous Soto Zen monk Ryokan (1756–1831), a great poet and calligrapher, who for a long time lived as a penniless vagrant. He writes that since practising the method of Master Hakuyu he no longer feels the winter's cold.

The atmosphere, and to some extent the ideal, of the main Yasenkanna text is Taoist. The Sennin is a mountain hermit living in retirement and knowing the secrets of immortality and of many psychic powers. In the preface, which is an important part of the document, the emphasis is shifted; it is ostensibly by a disciple of Hakuin, but strongly resembles the accounts of Naikan given in other works of Hakuin himself, and must in fact be by him.

There are numerous references to Chinese classics, whose immense prestige was almost always invoked when presenting ideas in Japan. The allusions to the ancient Book of Change require a note. The book is based on sixty-four hexagrams, in which an unbroken line stands for Yang, the positive light principle, and a broken line for Yin, the negative and dark. The hexagrams themselves are made up of two trigrams, each with

its own meaning. For instance hexagram No. 24 ䷗ consists of
☷ or Earth, with below it ☳ which stands for Thunder. The
whole hexagram thus is interpreted as thunder in the earth,
and in divination it is an omen of return. The related season is
winter, when below the earth the new life is latent. The hexagram is alluded to in our text as 'five Yins [i.e. broken lines]
above and one Yang [whole line] below'. Similarly No. 11 ䷊
has Earth ☷ above and Heaven ☰ below, that is: a mingling
which is interpreted as harmony. The hexagram is described
in the words 'three Yins above and three Yangs below'. This
explanation should resolve for the reader the apparent confusion in the number of Yins and Yangs.

Some other allusions to Chinese authorities mean little to
a Western reader; in certain cases I have compressed several
names into some phrase like 'sages of medicine'.

In Chinese alchemy, the elixir of immortality is Tan.
The word was used also in a psychophysical sense and in a
mystical sense. The field of the elixir is the Tanden, one inch
below the navel. In this region also is the energy-sea, variously
held either to be near or to include the Tanden. Concentration
on Tanden is a widespread doctrine in Far Eastern Buddhism
and in disciplines influenced by it.

Another important technical term is Ki, which originally
meant air; in this text it has its secondary meaning, something
akin to vital energy. When the notion comes to move the hand,
that is a function of Shin or heart; when the movement is ini-
tiated, that is a function of Ki. When Ki is sluggish or out of
harmony, the movements are clumsy and hesitant. Cultivation
of Ki, and especially unification of Ki and Shin with a view to
producing spontaneity of movement, was much studied by

fencers and others in Japan.

Phrases like 'metal of the lungs' refer to the distribution of the classical five Elements (fire, water, wood, metal and earth) among the five organs (heart, liver, etc.). The implications of the system are not important in following the text.

The So cream mentioned on page 158 was the purest of aliment; it was the food of the Sennin.

In some editions of Yasenkanna there is a second part, which is a letter developing the analogy between bodily health and the well-being of a country. It contains little of interest regarding Hakuin's spiritual development and is not translated here.

2. THE PREFACE
By a disciple, Cold Starveling, Master of Poverty Temple

In the year 1757, from a certain bookseller in the capital came to us a letter addressed to the personal attendants of Master Hakuin. After the usual greetings it said: 'I have heard that among the Master's papers there is a manuscript called Yasenkanna or some such title. In it is gathered together the lore of training Ki-energy, invigorating the spirit and fortifying the citadel, and in particular the alchemy of the Tan-elixir of the Sennin. To us dabblers in the world without, such news is a rainbow in a drought. We know that occasionally a copy is given privately to a student disciple, but they keep it as a secret treasure and never show it to others. So it is wasted, heavenly nectar locked away in the bookchest. What I now ask is new life to those bent with age, and relief to those that thirst. I have always heard that the Master makes it his delight to benefit the people, and this being of benefit to the people, why should the teacher begrudge it?'

The two tigers took this letter and presented it to the teacher, who smiled a little. But when we opened the book-chest some of the manuscript had been devoured by worms, only the middle part remaining. We completed it from our own private copies, the whole coming to some fifty pages. It has been bound and is ready to be sent to the capital. As senior by a day to the other disciples, the task of writing an introduction has fallen on me, and without more ado I begin it.

The teacher has been living at Shoinji temple a good forty years. Since he set up here, disciples have been coming. When they had crossed the threshold, the teacher's stinging words became sweet to them, and his blows were felt as kindness. They never thought of taking their leave; some for ten and some for twenty years, some dying – to become the dust under the branches of the temple pines – they never looked back. They were spiritual heroes and a glory to the world. For miles to the east and west, all the old houses and abandoned dwellings, ancient temples and ruined tombs, became lodging and abode for these pure ascetics.

Distress in the morning and hardship at even, starving by day and freezing at night, for food only raw vegetables and cornmeal; in their ears the master's blistering shouts and abuse, piercing their bones his furious fist and stick; at what they saw their foreheads furrowed, at what they heard their skins asweat. Angels would have shed tears and demons joined their palms in supplication. At the beginning fair to look on as Sogyoku or Ka-an, skin radiant and glistening with health, soon their form emaciated and face drawn, like the poets Toho or Koto, or like Kutsugen when he faced catastrophe at the Takuhan river. How would any have been held a moment longer, except the most valiant in the quest, who begrudged neither health nor life itself? But often the training became too much and the austerities excessive, so that their lungs were benumbed and their humours dried, with persistent pains and swelling in the abdomen, and chronic illnesses appearing.

Seeing that such sufferings were beyond even heroic endurance, the teacher turned down from the heights and pressed out the milk of mercy by giving them the secret of Naikan or inner contemplation. He said: 'When true students are pursuing the Way, the heart-fire may rush up to the head; body and mind become exhausted and the five organs lose their harmony. Against this condition not all the needles and cautery and drugs of the master doctors of China avail. But with me is the secret of the circulation of the Tanelixir of the Sennin, the immortal mountain sages. Do you now make trial of it. You feel the clouds and mists part and the sun appear in splendour.

'To practise the secret, for a while lay down the meditation practice and drop your Koan. The first thing is, that you must experience deep sleep. And before you shut your eyes to enter that sleep, stretch both legs right out and press them strongly together. Bring your whole vital energy to fill the energy-sea at the navel, the Tanden elixir-field, and the hips and legs and so right down to the soles of the feet. Again and again you must make this imagination:

> This the energy-sea, the Tanden, hips and legs down
>   to the soles, all is full of my Original Face.
> What nostrils would there be on that Face?
> This the energy-sea, the Tanden, is full of my true
> Home.
> What letter [needed] from that Home?
> This the energy-sea, the Tanden, is full of my Pure
>   Land of consciousness-only.
> What outer pomp for that Pure Land?
> This the energy-sea, the Tanden, is full of the Amida
> Buddha of this heart and body.
> What dharma would that Amida be preaching?

So repeating again and again, continuously make the mental pictures as described. As the practice begins to take effect, the hips and legs and right down to the soles will spontaneously become filled with Ki-energy. The abdomen below the navel will become rounded like a gourd or the smooth surface of a ball. If you again and again vividly make the visualisation in this way, after five or seven or at most twenty-one days, from the five organs and the six auxiliaries the exhaustion and fatigue and illnesses will be altogether swept away, and health will be restored. And if it be not so, you may cut off this head.'

All the disciples joyfully made salutations and set to practising the method in their own quarters. Everyone remarked a marvellous effect. The result depended on how well they did the practice, but most of them recovered completely. All the time we were telling each other about the miraculous effect of the Naikan.

The teacher said: 'O disciples, do not take it as enough just to recover from illness. The healthier you are, the more you must apply yourselves to spiritual practice; the more satori you get, the more you must press on. When I first entered on the path, I contracted a grave and refractory illness, whose agony was ten times what any of you have experienced. Desperate as I was, I came to feel that rather than live in such extreme misery it would be better to die quickly and throw off this sack of a body. But by great fortune I came to receive the secret of the Naikan, and recovered completely just as you have done.

'The Perfect Man [Hakuyu] told me: "This is the divine art of prolonging life possessed by the immortal Sennin. The lesser result is a life of three centuries, and as to the greater, it cannot be calculated." I myself rejoiced exceedingly when I heard it, and unflaggingly practised for some three years. I felt my mind and body steadily recover and my vitality steadily become vigorous. At this point I pondered again and again within, myself: suppose by this practice I can keep alive even eight centuries as did the patriarch Ho, yet it is only a prolonged emptiness, a preserved corpse void of intelligence, like an old fox hibernating in some ancient lair, only to die in the end. For how is it that today, of the company of the immortals Kakko, Tekkai, Choka, Hicho, not one is ever seen? Better to undertake the four universal vows, to devote myself to the glorious Bodhisattva path and practise the great dharma; am I to lose the body of Truth, which never dies even as space itself, which was not preceded even by space itself, in order to attain the imperishable diamond body of the Sennin?

'When I came here, I had by me one or two real inquirers, to whom I taught the Naikan and the Zen inquiry together. There was spiritual training and there was spiritual warfare, but in these thirty years new disciples have been coming in ones and twos each year, till today there are nearly two hundred of them. Some among them, exhausted and bowed with the training, had the heart-fire mounting to the head till they went almost mad with it, and I was moved to pass on to them privately the method of Naikan. They were cured then and there, and then with each enlightenment I urged them on more and more.

'I myself am now past seventy but have no trace of illness. My teeth are all sound, and over the clearness of sight and hearing never more than the slightest passing cloud. At the end of the regular fortnightly preaching of the dharma in the temple I feel no fatigue. I am asked from outside to lecture to groups of three to five hundred, and to expound the Sutras for periods of seven to ten weeks; I speak forcibly and directly, and altogether have given fifty or sixty such courses. Never did I miss a single day. I am well in body and mind, and my energy has gradually come far to surpass what it was at the age of twenty or thirty. Such is my own experience of the Naikan.'

We disciples made reverence with tears in our eyes at the greatness of what we had received from the teacher. We asked for permission to make a permanent record in book form of a summary of the method, that future disciples might be preserved from physical collapse. The teacher nodded, and the draft was at once prepared.

Now what does the book teach? It is this: the essential thing in replenishing the vitality and lengthening life is to invigorate the frame; the essential thing in invigorating the frame is to concentrate the spirit-energy at the Tanden in the energy-sea just below the navel. When the spirit is concentrated, the Ki-energy accumulates; when the Ki accumulates, the true Tan-elixir forms. When the elixir forms, the frame becomes firm; when the frame becomes firm the spirit is whole; when the spirit is whole the life is prolonged. This is the secret of the nine elixir-cycles of the Sennin. It must be understood that the elixir is not something external – the Tan is simply a question of taking the heart-fire downward to fill the Tanden below the navel. If students apply themselves to this essential point without falling away, the Zen illness will be cured and the body will be free from fatigue. Moreover, you will attain your Zen aspiration, and in years to come, entering the Great Questioning, will in the end be clapping your hands and laughing for joy. How so? As the moon rises, the castle shadows disappear.

3. YASENKANNA
by Hakuin

When as a beginner I entered on the Way, I vowed to practise with heroic faith and indomitable spirit. After a mere three years of strenuous effort, suddenly one night the moment came, when all my old doubts melted away down to their very roots. The age-old Karma-root of birth-and-death was erased utterly. I thought to myself: 'The way is never distant. Strange that the ancients spoke of twenty or thirty years, whereas I...' After some months lost in dancing joy, I looked at my life. The spheres of activity and stillness were not at all in harmony; I found I was not free to either take up a thing or leave it. I thought: 'Let me boldly plunge again into spiritual practice and once more throw away my life in it.' Teeth clenched and eyes aglare, I sought to free myself from food and sleep. Before a month had passed the heart-fire mounted to my head, my lungs were burning but my legs felt as if freezing in ice and snow. In my ears was a rushing sound as of a stream in a valley. My courage failed and I was in an attitude of constant fear. I felt spiritually exhausted, night and day seeing dreams, my armpits always wet with sweat and my eyes full of tears. I cast about in every direction, consulting famous teachers and doctors, but all their devices availed nothing at all.

Someone told me: 'In the mountains of the place called White-River, beyond the capital, there is one who dwells in the heights, known to the people as Master Hakuyu. He is believed to be over two hundred years old, and he lives there several miles from human habitation. He does not like to see people, and if they go he will run away and conceal himself Men do not know whether to think him a sage or a madman, but the villagers believe him to be a Sennin, one of the mountain immortals. They say he was once the teacher of Ishikawa Jozan, deeply versed in the science of the stars and the lore of medicine. Occasionally to a seeker who went in true reverence he has vouchsafed a word, which when pondered afterwards was of great benefit.'

So in the middle of January 1710, I quietly put together some travelling things, left Mino and crossed Black-Valley, finally coming to the village of White-River. Putting down my bundle in a teashop, I asked the whereabouts of the hermitage of Hakuyu. A villager directed me to a mountain stream in the far distance. I followed the rushing water, which took me to a remote mountain valley. Following straight up for a couple of miles, I found that it suddenly disappeared. There was no path and I was at a loss; unable to go on, I stood in dismay. Helplessly I sat down on a stone to one side, and with closed eyes and joined palms repeated a Sutra. As if by a miracle there came to my ears a distant sound of blows of an axe; pursuing the sound deeply into the trees, I came upon a woodcutter. The old man pointed towards the far-off mountain mists, and I made out a tiny patch of yellowish white, now concealed and now revealed by the movement of the haze – 'that is the reed curtain which hangs before the mouth of the cave of Master Hakuyu'. At once I tucked in my clothes and began to climb, now over steep rocks, now pushing through mountain grasses; my sandals soaked with snow and ice were freezing, and my clothes wet through with mist and dew. As I toiled on the sweat poured down, but gradually I came up to the place of the reed curtain. The exquisite purity of the landscape made me feel I had left the world of men. A dread shook my heart and soul, and I was shivering as if stripped naked.

I seated myself on a rock for a while and counted my breath up to some hundreds. Then I straightened and tidied my dress and went forward with reverent awe. Peering through the reed curtain, I dimly made out the form of Master Hakuyu, seated in meditation posture with his eyes closed. His hair streaked with white fell to his knees, his beautiful complexion was full and clear. A quilted cloth was thrown round him and his seat was a bed of soft grass. The cave was small, barely six foot square. There were no provisions of any kind, but on a low table three books: the Doctrine of the Mean, the classic of Lao Tzu, and the Diamond Sutra.

After making many salutations, I quietly related the course of my illness and asked for help. In a little he opened his eyes and looked at me keenly. He said slowly: 'I am just an ordinary man living out the rest of life in the mountains. I gather chestnuts for food and sleep in company with the tame deer. What do I know about anything else? I am only sorry that the journey in expectation of a holy man should have been in vain... I again and again repeated my reverences and my request. Then he quietly took my hand, made a careful examination of my condition and inspected the bodily openings. His long-nailed fingers smoothed his forehead in a gesture of sympathy: 'Your condition is pitiable. By contemplating on truth too strenuously, you have lost the rhythm of spiritual advance, and that has finally brought on a grievous malady. And it is something very hard to cure, this Zen illness of yours. Though the sages of medicine frown over your case and put forth all their skill with needle and cautery and drugs, yet would they be help-less. You have been broken by your contemplation on truth (Ri-kan), and unless you devote yourself to inner contemplation (Nai-kan) you can never recover. There is a saying that you rise by means of that same ground on which you fell, and the Naikan method is an example of that principle.'

I said: 'Be gracious enough to tell me the secret of the Naikan, and I will practise it in the temple.'

His face became solemn, his appearance changed and he began to speak slowly: 'So. You are a real seeker. Shall I pass on to you a little of what I heard long ago? It is the secret of replenishing life, and those who know it are few. If you practise it without falling away, you will surely see a marvel-lous effect in yourself, and it may well be that you will never close your eyes in death.

'The great Way (Tao) dividing itself, there are the two prin-ciples Yin and Yang, by whose mingling in harmony are born men and things. In man the primal Ki-energy moves silently in the centre, and the five organs range themselves and the pulse moves. The supporting Ki-energy and the nourishing blood move in a circulation, rising and falling, about fifty cycles in the course of one day and night. The lungs, under the metal sign, are feminine and float above the diaphragm; the liver, under the wood sign, is masculine and is sunk below the diaphragm. The heart–fire–is the sun, the great Yang, with its place above, and the kidneys–water–are the great Yin, occupying the lower place. In the five organs are seven divinities, the spleen and the kidneys having each two. The outbreath goes from the heart and lungs, the inbreath comes to the kidneys and liver. With each outbreath the pulse current advances three inches, and at each inbreath another three. In a day and night there are 13,500 breaths and the pulse makes the circuit of the body fifty times. Fire is light and buoyant, ever inclined to ascend; water is heavy and always tends downwards.

'If you do not know these things, your efforts at contemplation lose the rhythm and the will becomes over-extended; then the heart-fire blazing up strikes the metal of the lungs which is scorched and impaired. As the metal mother (lungs) suffers, the water child (kidneys) decays and dies. Parent and child are injured, all five organs are afflicted and the six auxiliaries oppressed. The elements losing their harmony produce a hundred and one diseases. Against this condition all remedies lose their power, and though every art of medicine be enlisted, in the end they can claim no success.

'Replenishing the life is in fact like looking after a kingdom. The bright lord, the sage ruler, always concentrates his heart on those below; the dull lord, the ordinary ruler, is always letting his heart go upward as it wills. And when it flies up at its own will, the great nobles become overbearing and the minor officials rely on special favours, and no one of them ever looks down at the misery of the masses. In the country the peasants are emaciated, the land starves, the people die. Wisdom and virtue hide themselves and the masses are full of resentment and hate. The nobles become independent and rebellious, and strife arises with barbarian enemies. The people are reduced to the last extremity; the life-pulse of the country becomes sluggish and finally extinct.

'But when the ruler concentrates his heart downwards, the great nobles check their ostentation, the minor officials carry out their duties, and the labour of the people never goes unrewarded. The farmers have abundant crops and their women clothes; many wise men are attracted into service with the ruler, the retainers are respectful and obedient, the people prosperous and the country strong. None within conspires to defeat the law, and no enemy attacks the frontiers. The country does not hear the sound of war and the people need know nothing of weapons.

'It is just so with the human body. The perfect man always keeps the lower regions filled with his heart-energy; when the heart energy is thus made full downwards, the seven ills find no place within and assaults from without find no weak point. The body is vigorous and robust and the heart-spirit sound. So the mouth never knows the taste of medicines, sweet or bitter, the body never has to undergo the pains of cautery and needle. But the ordinary man takes the heart-energy always freely upwards, and when it thus mounts as it likes, the (heart) fire on the left overcomes the (lung) metal on the right, the senses dwindle and fail and the six auxiliaries are oppressed and lose their harmony. So it is that Shitsuen says: "The true man breathes his breath from the heels, the ordinary man breathes his breath from the throat." Kyoshun says: "When the Ki is in the lower region, the breath is long; when it is in the upper region, the breath is contracted." Joyoshi says: "In man the energy is verily one alone. When it goes down to the Tanden, the Yang reacts, and the beginning of the reaction in the form of Yang can be confirmed by a feeling of warmth." The general rule for replenishing the life is that the upper regions should be always cool and the lower regions warm.

'The pulses of the body are twelve-branched, corresponding to the twelve months of the year and the twelve periods of the day. So also the Book of Change has its six seasons, whose cycle of change makes up the year. In this system, when five Yins are above and one Yang is held below, the omen is *Thunder in the earth returning*. The reference is to the depth of winter, and this is what is meant by the true man's breathing from the heels. When three Yangs are in the lower position and three Yins above, it is *Earth and Heaven in harmony*, the season of the new year when everything is imbued with life-bearing energy and the plants receive the abundance for the spring blossoming. This represents the perfect man's taking down his energy to fill the lower regions, and when a man attains it he is filled with heroic vigour. But when five Yins are below and one Yang remains above, it is *Mountain and Earth stripped*, the season of September. When it manifests in nature, forest and garden lose their colours and all the plants fade and fall. The ordinary man's breathing from the throat is a symbol of it. In the human body it is a drying and stiffening of the frame, with the teeth becoming loose and falling. Of this condition the books on prolonging life say that the six Yangs are all exhausted – in other words the man who is only Yin is near death. What has to be known is just this: the central principle is to take the life energy down to fill the lower regions.

'In olden times Tokeisho purified himself before appearing in front of the teacher Sekidai to ask about the secret of distilling the Tan-elixir. The teacher said: "I have the secret of the great mystic elixir, but there is no transmission except to one of superior merit." Again in antiquity, when Koseishi transmitted it to the Yellow Emperor, the Emperor had to perform purification for twenty-one days in order to be fit to receive it. Apart from the great Tao there is no elixir, and apart from the elixir no great Tao. Now there is a method of fivefold purification: when the six cravings are abandoned, and the five senses have forgotten their operation, you will dimly perceive filling you the life-energy, hard to distinguish. This is what the Taoist Taihaku meant when he said: "Through the divine energy in me to unite with the primal divine energy."'

'Mencius speaks of the free energy in man. This is to be led to the Tanden in the energy-sea at the navelwheel and concentrated there; for months and years protect it and maintain the unity, nourish it and make it perfect. One morning that alchemist's crucible will suddenly be transcended, and within and without and in the middle, in all directions and in everything, there will be the one great elixir circulating. Then at last you awaken and attain to the self, the true immortality of the great spiritual Sennin, which was not born even before heaven and earth were, which does not die even after space itself has ceased to exist. In the alchemy of the Tan-elixir this is the season of *Fulfilment*. Why do they cling to little psychic powers like riding on the wind and bestriding the mists, crushing the earth and walking on water, churning the ocean to produce the celestial So cream and transmuting clay into yellow gold? A sage has said: "The Tan-elixir is the Tanden, just below the navel. The secret alchemical liquid is that from the lungs, which is to be taken and returned to the Tanden." So the teaching is, the metal liquid is the circulation of the Tan.'

I said: 'With reverence I hear. I am to drop my Zen contemplation for a while, and cure myself by devoting my time to these new practices. I have one misgiving: may this not be what Rishisai condemns as falling into pure inertia? If the heart is held to one place, will not the Ki and the blood become stagnant?'

Hakuyu smiled a little and replied: 'Not so. Does not Rishisai say that the nature of fire is to blaze up and therefore it should be taken down, whereas the nature of water is to sink and therefore it should be made to rise? Water ascending and fire descending, that is what he calls the mixing. When they are mixed the omen is *Fulfilled*; when they are unmixed the omen is *Unfulfilled*. The former is the sign of life, the latter the sign of death. The school of Rishisai condemns the so-called sinking into pure inertia in order to save students from falling into the error of Tankei (who cultivates only the Yin).

'An ancient says: "The minister-fire tends to rise and oppress the body; remedy this with water which by nature controls fire." The fire indeed is of dual nature, the prince-fire which is above and has charge of stillness, and the minister-fire which is below and has charge of activity. The princefire is the lord of the heart, the minister-fire is its servant. The minister-fire itself is dual, namely kidneys and liver. The liver is compared to thunder and the kidneys to dragons. So it is said, *when the dragons are taken back to the bottom of the sea, thunder will not break forth, and when the thunder is taken into concealment in the depths of the lake, the dragons will not soar aloft*. Sea and lake are both of watery nature; this is the secret of preventing the tendency of the minister-fire to mount. Again it is said: "When the heart is exhausted, in the vacuity fire blazes up; therefore at the time when there is vacuity, take the fiery energy down-wards and mingle it with the kidneys – that is the remedy." It is the way of *Fulfilment*.

'From the mounting of the heart-fire your grievous illness has arisen. If you do not take it down you will never recover, though you learn and practise all the healing remedies human and divine. Now it may be that as my outward appearance is that of a Taoist, you fancy that my teaching is far from Buddhism. But this is Zen. One day, when you break through, you will see how laughable were your former ideas.

'This contemplation attains right contemplation by no-contemplation. Many-pointed contemplation is wrong contemplation. Hitherto your contemplation has been many-pointed and so you have contracted this grave malady. Is it not then proper to cure it by no-contemplation? If you now control the fire of heart and will and put it in the Tanden and right down to the soles of the feet, your breast will of itself become cool, without a thought of calculation, without a ripple of passion. This is true contemplation, pure contemplation. Do not call it dropping your Zen contemplation, for the Buddha himself says: "Hold your heart down in the soles of the feet and you heal a hundred and one ills." Further the Agama scriptures speak of the use of the So cream in curing mental exhaustion. The Tendai meditation classic called "Stopping and Contemplating" deals in detail with illnesses and their causes, and describes the methods of treatment. It gives twelve different ways of breathing to cure various forms of illness, and it prescribes the method of visualising a bean at the navel. The main point is always that the heart-fire must be taken down and kept at the Tanden and down to the soles, and this not only cures illness but very much helps Zen contemplation.

'In the Tendai system there are in fact two forms of Stopping: one is by controlling the associations, and the other is clearness of Truth. The latter is full contemplation of reality, whereas the former stresses first restraining the mind and vitality in the Tanden. If the student practises it, he will find it most useful. Long ago the Zen patriarch Dogen, founder of Eiheiji temple, crossed to China and made his reverence before the teacher Nyojo on Mount Tendo. One day he entered the master's room and asked for instruction. The master said: "O Dogen, at the time of sitting in meditation, put your heart on your left palm." This is fundamentally what the Tendai master means by his Stopping. The latter records in one of his works on the subject how he taught the secret to a sick brother, whom it saved from death.

'Again, Abbot Haku-un says: "I always direct my heart so that it fills my abdomen. Helping students or receiving visitors or entertaining guests, however it may be, preaching or teaching and all else, I have never ceased to do it. Now in my old age the virtue of the practice is clearly apparent." This is well said indeed. It is based on the phrase in the Somon classic of medicine: "When you are quiet and simple, and empty within, the true Ki-energy conforms to that. If the spirit is kept within, how should sickness come?" The point is to keep the fundamental Ki within, pervading and supporting the whole body so that in the 360 joints and 84,000 pores there is not a hair's breadth without it. Know this to be the secret of preserving life.

'Master Ho (who lived 800 years) speaks thus of a method of harmonising the spirit and directing the Ki: "Shut yourself away in a quiet private room, and prepare a bed level and warm, with a pillow two-and-a-half inches high. Stretch yourself out on the back, close the eyes and confine the heart energy within the breast. Put a feather on the nose and make your breathing so slow that it is not moved. After three hundred breaths the ears hear nothing, the eyes see nothing; in this state heat and cold cannot assail, the bee's sting cannot poison. Life will be prolonged to 360 years and you approach the state of the immortals."

'The great poet-mystic Sotoba says: "Do not eat till you are hungry, and stop before you are satisfied. Go for a walk until the exertion makes the stomach empty, and when it is empty enter a quiet room. Sit silently in the meditation posture and count the outgoing and incoming breaths. Count from one to ten, from ten to a hundred, from a hundred to a thousand, when the body will become immobile and the heart serene as the clear sky. If this practice is prolonged, the breath will come to a stop of itself. When it neither comes in nor goes out, a vaporous exhalation will come from the 84,000 pores, rising like a mist. You find that all illnesses you ever had are removed, and every obstacle eliminated. Now, like a blind man whose eyes have suddenly been opened, you do not need to ask another the way." The only thing needed is to cut short worldly talk and build up the fundamental Ki. So it is said: He who would nourish the power of the eyes always keeps them shut, he who would nourish the power of the ears is never eager to hear, he who would nourish the heart-energy is ever silent.'

I asked: 'May I hear of the use of the So cream?' Hakuyu said: 'If the student finds in his meditation that the four great elements are out of harmony, and body and mind are fatigued, he should rouse himself and make this meditation. Let him visualise placed on the crown of his head that celestial So ointment, about as much as a duck's egg, pure in colour and fragrance. Let him feel its exquisite essence and flavour melting and filtering down through his head, its flow permeating downwards, slowly laving the shoulders and elbows, the sides of the breast and within the chest, the lungs, liver, stomach and internal organs, the back and spine and hip bones. All the old ailments and adhesions and pains in the five organs and six auxiliaries follow the mind downwards. There is a sound as of the trickling of water. Percolating through the whole body, the flow goes gently down the legs, stopping at the soles of the feet.

'Then let him make this meditation: that the elixir having permeated and filtered down through him, its abundance fills up the lower half of his body. It becomes warm, and he is saturated in it. Just as a skilful physician collects herbs of rare fragrance and puts them in a pan to boil, so the student feels that from the navel down he is simmering in the So elixir. When this meditation is being done there will be psychological experiences, of a sudden indescribable fragrance at the nose-tip, of a gentle and exquisite sensation in the body. Mind and body become harmonised and far surpass their condition at the peak of youth. Adhesions and obstructions are cleared away, the organs are tranquillised and insensibly the skin begins to glow. If the practice is carried on without relapse, what illness will not be healed, what power will not be acquired, what perfection will not be attained, what Way will not be fulfilled? The arrival of the result depends only on how the student performs the practices.

'When I was a youth I was much more ill than you are now. The doctors gave up the case, and I clutched at a hundred expedients but could find no art that would help me. I prayed to the deities of heaven and earth, and invoked the aid of the divine Sennin. By their grace there came to me unexpectedly the secret of the So cream. My joy was indescribable, and I practised it continuously. Before a month had passed the greater part of the illnesses had been eliminated, and thereafter I have felt only lightness and peace in my body and mind. Unmoving, unwinding, I do not reckon the months nor keep track of the years; thoughts of the world have become few, old habits and desires seem forgotten. I do not know how old I may be. For a time I came to wander in solitude in the mountains of Wakasu; that was about thirty years. No one in the world knew me. When I look back it is just like the dream at Koryan (where a traveller dreamed the events of a lifetime in half an hour). Now, alone in these mountains, I have set free this body. There are only a couple of cloths for covering, yet in the hardest winter, when the cloth curls under the cold, my body suffers no chill. The grain comes to an end and often there is nothing to eat for several months, yet I feel neither hunger nor cold. What is this but the power of the Naikan? The secret I have given you is something whose mysteries you will never exhaust. Besides this, what have I to tell you?'

He closed his eyes and sat in silence. My eyes were full of tears as I made my farewell salutations.

Slowly I descended from the cave mouth. The remaining sunbeams just touched the tips of the trees. I began to notice a sound of footsteps echoing in the mountain and valley. An awe and dread came over me, and fearfully I turned to look back. I saw in the distance that the Master Hakuyu had left the rock cave. As he came up he said: 'In these trackless mountains you can easily be lost. I will guide your steps lest you get into difficulties.' With his great wooden clogs and thin staff he trod the steep rocks and sheer cliffs lightly as level ground; talking and laughing he showed me the way. Two or three miles down the mountain we came to the valley stream. He said: 'Follow its course and you come safe to White-River valley,' and abruptly left me. For some time I stood like a tree, watching the master returning, his stride like that of an ancient hero. So lightly he escaped the world, ascending the mountain as if on wings. A longing and an awe were on me – to the end of my days I have regretted that I could not follow such a man.

Slowly I went back. I absorbed myself continuously in the Naikan practices, and in barely three years all my maladies disappeared of themselves without drugs or other treatment. Not merely was the illness cured, but the Koan, hard to hold and hard to follow, hard to understand and hard to enter, on which before I could find no purchase for hand or foot, into which I could not bite, now I followed to the root and penetrated to the bottom. Six or seven times I had the great bliss of that passing through, and times without counting the dancing joy of minor satori. I knew that the old master Daiye was verily not deceiving us when he spoke of eighteen great satori realisations and countless lesser ones.

As for myself, in the old days the soles of my feet were always freezing as if in ice, even when I wore two or three pairs of socks, but now during the three months of winter's rigour I neither put on socks nor warm my feet at the fire. I have passed my seventieth year, yet there is no trace of illness to be found, and surely this is the effect of the divine secret.

Now let it not be said that the old dodderer of Shoinji has with his dying gasps chronicled a mass of drivel to bamboozle good men. For those who are already spiritual ashes, whose blow has struck through to satori, for those higher ones this was never meant; but to dullards like myself, who have been ill like me, it will undoubtedly be of help if studied. The only fear is that outsiders may clap their hands and laugh over it. When the horse is chewing up an old straw basket, one can't get a nap in peace.

Part Three

The Tiger's Cave

and Other Pieces

The Lotus in the Mire
Poems by Zen master Mamiya
The Dance of the Sennin
Maxims of Saigo

The world when self is lost – Laotzu, Buddha, Confucius

1. THE TIGER'S CAVE

The Shogun Iemitsu, in early seventeenth-century Japan, was very interested in fencing, and kept several fencing masters at his court. Also in favour was the Zen master Takuan, from whom many of these masters took lessons in meditation and Zen.

A wild tiger was sent from Korea to the Shogun as a present, and when the caged animal was being admired, the Shogun suggested to the renowned fencer Yagiu that he enter the cage and use the arts of fencing to approach the tiger and stroke its head. In spite of the warnings of the tiger's keeper, Yagiu went into the cage with only a fan. Holding the fan before him he fixed his gaze on the tiger and slowly advanced. In face of the animal's threatening growls he managed to hold it under a psychological dominance and just to touch its head. Then he slowly retreated and escaped from the cage. As he came out the sweat poured off him.

The Shogun turned to Takuan and said: 'Has Zen anything else to show?' The Zen master ran down to the cage, his sleeves flying in the wind. He jumped into the cage and faced the tiger. The master spat on his palm and held it out to the tiger, which sniffed and then licked his hand. The master lightly touched its head, then turned and softly jumped out of the cage.

'After all,' marvelled the Shogun, 'our way of the sword cannot compete with Zen.'

* * *

When a rebel army swept into a town in Korea, all the monks of the Zen temple fled except for the Abbot. The general came into the temple and was annoyed that the Abbot did not receive him with respect. 'Don't you know,' he shouted, 'that you are looking at a man who can run you through without blinking?'

'And you,' replied the Abbot strongly, 'are looking at a man who can be run through without blinking!' The general stared at him, then made a bow and retired.

* * *

Kasuisai is one of the important temples of the Soto sect in Japan, and the name means a place for sleeping. This strange name derives from an incident after the civil wars in Japan, during which the temple had given refuge to fleeing warriors of both sides, in spite of warnings not to do so.

After Ieyasu had established himself as effective ruler of Japan, he rode up to the temple in order to settle accounts with the Abbot. His retinue of warriors made it clear that he intended to revenge himself.

He sent in a message to the Abbot to present himself immediately. The boy came back with a message that the Abbot was feeling sleepy, and would the Shogun come back some other time.

Ieyasu bowed his head in respect and rode away.

* * *

Cleaning: work is done with enthusiasm

Dance of the Sennin

During the civil disturbances in the nineteenth century a fugitive samurai took refuge in the temple of Soto Zen master Bokusan. Three pursuers arrived and demanded to know where he was. 'No one here,' said the Zen master. 'If you won't tell us, then let's cut off your head,' and they drew their swords to do so. 'Then if I am to die,' said the Zen master, 'I think I'll have a little wine.' And he took down a small bottle, poured it, and sipped with evident relish.

The samurai looked at one another. Finally they went away.

Bokusan was repeatedly asked about this incident, but did not want to discuss it. Once however he said: 'Well, there is something to be learnt from it. When those fellows came, I did not do what they wanted, but neither did I quarrel with them or plead with them. I just gave up their whole world and had nothing to do with them. And after a time I found they had gone away.

'Similarly when people complain that they are over-whelmed with passions and wrong thoughts, they should know that the right way is not to quarrel nor to plead or argue. Simply give up all claim on their world and have nothing to do with them, and after a time you will find that they have gone away.'

* * *

Zen masters did not every time go unscathed. One of the greatest figures in Chinese Zen, Ganto of the Tang dynasty, always told his disciples: 'When I go, I shall go with a great shout.' Brigands invaded the place and all fled the temple except Abbot Ganto, who remained quietly in his quarters. A brigand came and demanded food; when the Abbot could not supply it he ran him through. The Abbot gave a great shout which was heard for miles, and died.

This incident was a formidable obstacle to Hakuin in Japan many centuries later; all his doubts crystallised round the death of Ganto. When illumination finally came he cried: 'I am Ganto, unharmed!' (See page 135 of this book.)

* * *

Daito, one of the great lights of Rinzai Zen in Japan, for many years lived unknown among the beggars of Kyoto. At this time there was a barbarous habit of testing a new sword on a man; some degraded samurai used to take a new sword out and try it on a beggar. One such man appeared near the bridge where the beggars congregated, and all were terrified, knowing that when evening came he would probably appear among them and cut a man down.

The Zen master told the others to hide, and when the samurai appeared on the bridge at dusk he saw a beggar sitting in meditation posture. He drew his sword and shouted: 'Get ready, my sword is going to make two of you!' The beggar remained unmoving. An awe came over the samurai; he hesitated and then beat a retreat.

* * *

Shoju, teacher of Hakuin, practised his meditation sitting in the face of death. He came upon a village which had been invaded by wolves so that the inhabitants had fled. He sat in meditation throughout the night; he felt a wolf put its paws on his shoulders and growl into his face, but remained without moving. He recommended such practices to his pupils as the only means of knowing whether they had overcome identification with the illusory self of body-mind.

* * *

Muso Kokushi, teacher of emperors, was one of the spiritual giants of the Rinzai transmission in Japan. Once he and a lay follower, who was an expert fencer, were crossing a river together. The layman took the baggage and the master, as it happened, sat on the other side of the ferry-boat. The boat filled up and the boatman was turning away passengers when a drunken samurai rushed up and demanded to be taken on board. The boatman was afraid to refuse. In the dangerously overloaded boat the samurai began to start a quarrel; the Zen master intervened and pointed out that any violent movement might sink the boat.

'Meddling priest!' shouted the drunken man, and hit him on the forehead with his iron war-fan. The blood poured down. The master sat unmoving and the samurai, satisfied, slumped in his own place without further disturbance.

The boat reached the other shore, and the fencer lightly jumped out, looking steadily at the samurai and waiting for him to come ashore. There is something about the posture of an expert with the sword which is unmistakable; the bully had enough experience to know that he was going to pay with his life for having struck the friend of a master swordsman.

But Muso came forward quickly and said: 'No! Now, now is the time to apply our Buddhism. These forms are Emptiness; anger and all the passions are the Bodhi.' And he led his follower quietly away.

2. THE LOTUS IN THE MIRE

In times of famine, daughters of farmers allowed themselves to be sold to brothels in order to save the family. They took it as a sacrifice and did not lose their self-respect. Prostitutes were known as 'lotuses in the mire'.

Takuan was asked to write a poem on the picture of a prostitute. He wrote:

The Buddha sells the doctrine;
The patriarchs sell the Buddha;
The great priests sell the patriarchs;
She sells her body, –
That the passions of all beings may be quieted.
Form is Emptiness, the passions are the Bodhi.

On another picture, of Bodhidharma facing a prostitute, was written:

Against your sagehood what can I put except sincerity?

* * *

Zen master Mokudo when passing through the capital Edo was hailed by a prostitute from a second-storey window. He asked how she knew his name and she replied: 'When you were a boy on the farm we were neighbours; after you became a monk there was a bad harvest, and so I am here.' He went up and talked to her and she asked him to stay the night.

He paid her fee to the house, and gave some more to her. They talked of their families till late, and then the bedding was spread and she prepared to go to bed. He sat in meditation posture. She plucked his sleeve and said: 'You have been so kind, and I should like to show my appreciation. No one know.'

He said to her: 'Your business is sleeping, and my business is sitting. Now you get on with your sleeping, and I'll get on with my sitting!' And he remained unmoving the whole night.

* * *

A well-known doctor in the twentieth century was a good amateur potter, and sometimes had parties of his patients at which he showed them his work. Once he invited a Zen master whom he knew slightly. The master arrived as a small bowl was being passed round, and they waited for his opinion. He looked round solemnly and said:

'If any of you are ill in the future, I advise you not to call in this man. Because he must be a terrible doctor!'

There was a dead silence. Then one old man asked: 'But why, master?'

'His heart's not in his medicine, that's why. Look at this bowl. Oh, it's well enough, no doubt, but not up to professional standards, so even as a bowl it doesn't really stand. And this man – he collects patients simply so that he can show them his pots!'

The doctor took it to heart and abandoned the artist's vanity which had taken such a deep hold and was impairing his study of medicine.

* * *

At one point in a Zen funeral service, the priest has to give the traditional Katsu! shout. This expresses his realisation, and affects the condition of the departed.

On one occasion a father had a disturbing dream after the funeral of his daughter, and went to see the priest. 'Where is my daughter?' he demanded. 'What do you mean?' said the priest. 'You gave the Katsu! – now tell me, what is the condition of my daughter now?' shouted the father. The priest could not reply.

He gave up his temple and returned to the training monastery to find the secret of the shout.

* * *

The daughter of a rich merchant fell seriously ill, and she asked her father to request a famous Zen master to visit her.

The master demanded a fee of fifty gold pieces. The merchant was furious but at last agreed. The master came and told the girl: 'With these gold pieces we are going to build a new meditation hall. Among the monks are two or three baby

Bodhisattvas, and in that hall they train and come to maturity. Now you can die if you like; your life has had some meaning.' And he abruptly left.

At once she began to recover.

3. POEMS BY ZEN MASTER MAMIYA

(Japan, early twentieth century)

Sometimes there is the opportunity
   But not the capital;
Sometimes there is the capital
   But not the opportunity;
Rarely, very rarely, come at the same time
   Opportunity and capital both –
But then I am not there myself.
   Oh this world!

*

A gentleman came to see me
With talk of a remarkable investment.
'Sir, I am a penniless priest;
All I can give is the treasure of satori
Which ends sufferings for ever ...'
But he had left,
But he had left.

On a lotus leaf sits a frog,
His hands folded, his mind still,
In meditation.
Look out, look out!
Behind him a hungry snake,
Searching for food, is putting out its tongue.
Does he know? Does he not know? The frog
Sits in meditation with closed eyes.
Look out, look out!

4. THE DANCE OF THE SENNIN

In China and Japan there is a tradition that certain spiritually enlightened sages live in the mountains, enjoying unbroken freedom and delight. They do not encourage disciples or give formal instruction, but their mere existence purifies the soul of the world. There is a traditional dance sometimes performed on the Kabuki stage in Japan, which expresses something of the inner life of two famous Sennin or mountain sages. The accompanying song was written by a Buddhist priest. Kanzan and his friend Jittoku were spiritual 'lunatics' who lived in China in the Tang dynasty well over a thousand years ago; the former was a well-known poet, and some of his poems still survive. In many paintings he is shown with a scroll. Jittoku (the name means 'foundling') was found abandoned at the gate of a monastery. He lived on scraps of food, and used to carry a broom with which he swept the gardens of the monastery.

The curtain goes up on the two Sennin, posed as in one of the famous pictures of them. The backcloth is copied from a landscape by Sesshu; does it mean that in the eye of the Sennin the whole of nature is an artistic masterpiece? Kanzan, an elderly austere figure, is holding an unrolled scroll before him; it is his latest poem. Jittoku, much younger, leans on his broom, smiling secretly to himself. Slowly they begin to move; the steps are not the classical steps of any dance. As Jittoku slowly whirls his long sleeves in circles in the air, looking at them fascinated, it has the artless charm and grace of a very young child fully concentrated on waving a rag. His black hair falls down over his shoulders without any restriction, his absorbed face has no lines of anxiety or effort, his posture shows unconscious serenity and ease.

Kanzan has rolled up the scroll and stands abstracted, looking into infinity. The other seems struck by the dignity of the pose, and joining his hands in prayer walks round him in the traditional Eastern ceremonial manner. Completing the circle, he kneels before him with great reverence, his upturned face showing the perfect trust of the devotee, the perfect confidence of an infant in his parent. Kanzan slowly brings his gaze downward, and realising what the other wants, kneels beside him and unrolls the scroll. Together they are reading the poem; the scroll is held before them and we cannot see the writing, but we do see their eyes travelling down the first line and on to the next. There is some phrase here of genius; they stop reading to exchange a significant glance, slowly nodding their heads as if to say: 'A perfect expression!' They go back to their reading, and in mounting excitement rise together, still holding the scroll in front of them. As they turn away we see that it is perfectly blank. Kanzan rolls the scroll again; Jittoku smiles to himself as he picks up his broom.

The dance continues – the words of the song become wilder. Jittoku fetches the wine-gourd, but he has let the stopper fall and is holding it upside down. No wine – but, never mind, he fills it from the mountain stream and they savour it together. Cause and effect have ceased to operate in these high regions: gradually they become tipsy – Kanzan can hardly stand and the other has to support him. They would lapse into unconsciousness but a bird calls sweetly and distracts their attention from the drinking bout.

They resume the original pose, Kanzan with the scroll and Jittoku the broom. On Kanzan's austere features we see the beginnings of a smile, and now Jittoku looks full at us and begins to laugh silently. Is he laughing at us, or with us? The curtain comes across with a rush and we are left lost in our thoughts.

5. MAXIMS OF SAIGO

Takamori Saigo, known to all Japanese as 'Great Saigo', was a samurai who played a leading part in Japan's history at the end of last century. He took an active part in the overthrow of the feudal government and the establishment of a constitutional government, based on Western models.

He became Foreign Minister in the new government, and brought to its support his tremendous personal prestige and strength of character. Later he resigned on a point of principle and went into retirement. In 1876, his clan organised a rebellion against what they considered the mistaken policy of the government in foreign affairs, and Saigo was called in to lead it. The rebellion failed, and Saigo, as a final protest, killed himself in the traditional manner of the samurai.

Saigo was a man of heavy build. His friends affectionately nicknamed him 'The Bull'. He was famous for his personal bravery; his courage and endurance were shown by the fact that a year's imprisonment and torture by the feudal party could not break him. As Foreign Minister he won the respect of all for his complete frankness and sincerity. He lived a life of extreme austerity even at the height of his worldly success. He is said to have possessed only one kimono – while this was washed, the Foreign Minister received no callers.

Like many samurai of his time, Saigo studied Zen Buddhism under a great master. The aphorisms here translated crystallise the experience of his life. The thought is derived from Zen and from the philosophy of the Chinese Confucian sage, Wang Yang Ming.

One who wants neither life, nor name, nor rank, nor money, is hardly to be controlled. It is only such indomitable men who can carry great affairs of state through adversities to completion.

Do not have dealings with men; make your dealings with Heaven. In this way, confronting Heaven, put forth your whole endeavour. Never lay blame on other men, but consider where your own sincerity falls short.

In matters great and small tread the way of righteousness, apply complete sincerity, and never once use trickery. Many resort to it when they meet an obstacle, thinking that if just this one obstacle can be got round, they will be able to carry on somehow. But the disasters attendant on trickery inevitably arise, and the project always fails. The path of righteousness may not seem the shortest at first, but one who treads it quickly achieves success.

The Way being natural to the Universe, man as a follower of the Way should make it his purpose to revere Heaven. Heaven loves others and myself in the same way, and with that heart which loves me, loves others also.

One who follows the Way meets difficulties in the course of things, but however grave the situation, he never cares at all for success and failure or whether he live or die.

People think these days that if they only have sufficient cleverness, things turn out as they wish, but I find it most dangerous to trust to cleverness.

Deceiving others and plotting in secret, even supposing it to succeed, is the depth of depravity in a wise man. Behave towards others with justice and sincerity. Without justice one can never be a hero.

After setting right a mistake, it is best just to think: 'This mistake was made by me.' Then, putting the matter away and not turning back, pass on at once. To feel mortified over a mistake and worry about how to gloss it over, is as useless as to try to mend a smashed teacup.

The Way is the natural way of the Universe, and to learn it, one must revere Heaven, love man, and live one's life from first to last in self-control. As a rule men succeed by self-control, and fail through self-love. Study the lives of the men of this and other ages. When a man sets about something, he generally completes seven- or eight-tenths of it, but rarely completely succeeds with the remaining two-tenths. This is because, at the beginning, a man fully restrains his egoity and respects the work for itself. Results begin to come, and his fame increases. But then egoity stirs, the prudent and restrained attitude is relaxed, pride and boasting flourish. In the confidence born of his achievements so far, he plans to complete the work for his own ends. But his efforts have become bungling, and the end is failure – all invited by himself. Therefore restrain the self, and be careful not to heed what others do or say.

What is admired by the world and posterity is simply one moment of complete sincerity. Even if it does happen that the world praises a man of no sincerity, it is praising a mere fluke. But where there is great sincerity, then, even if none know that man in his own day, surely in after ages there will be those who know him.

Part Four

Zen

by Rosen Takashina
Primate of the Soto Zen Sect

In one morning as associations come,
He assumes the form of bodhisattva or devil

1. THE SERMON OF NO WORDS

There is an ancient saying: 'Better an inch of practice than a foot of preaching.' It refers to the sermon preached by the body itself, through action and without speaking.

The sermon of words and phrases is the finger pointing to the moon, the fist knocking at the door. The object is to see the moon not the finger, to get the door open and not the knocking itself; so far as these things do achieve their objects they are well. The object of the Buddha's life of preaching was not to turn words and phrases. The Diamond Sutra compares his sermons to a raft, which is only an instrument for reaching the far shore. The sermon which is an instrument can be discarded after a time, but the real preaching –which is not discarded – is the preaching by the body itself.

As to what that preaching may be, the truth of it is very profound, but in simple language it means that others receive right inspiration from that man. It is said that when a Bodhisattva has continued his spiritual practice for three kalpa-ages he is qualified to be a Buddha. After a hundred ages, his appearance becomes majestic. This does not mean anything outwardly magnificent, but it means that in helping others the manner in which the thing is done is of first importance, and through the force of his wisdom and compassion there manifests in him a peculiar dignity and tenderness. By contemplating the form of Bodhisattvas like Kannon and Jizo, one's heart becomes somehow softened, but along with that there is something awe-inspiring which cannot be gainsaid. When a man feels it within him all the time, it is naturally reflected in his outward appearance, and love and respect are attracted to him from others.

What gives us inspiration is the sermon of action of the Bodhisattva. He has the power to do it without uttering a word. But it is not to be confined to Buddhas and Bodhisattvas. For religious and other teachers, for all who stand in authority whether over many, as head of a household with many dependants, or as employer of a single man or girl, it is all-important.

A sermon is not something said by the Buddha long ago, or prated nowadays from a pulpit. The sermon of words is like a sort of advertising puff; but the real sermon is when the employer acts as a right employer, the servant as a right servant, and so with the merchant and official. All things, dogs and cats, trees and grass, things animate and inanimate, have all so to say their right path, and, so far as they keep to it without faltering, it is the sermon of action.

A poem of Sontoku expresses it: Without voice or incense, heaven and earth are ever repeating the unwritten scripture.

The man called Reiun was realised when he saw the peach blossoms; the man Kyogen when he heard a stone strike against a bamboo. There are instances of men who having matured their spiritual training were then enlightened on seeing the flying petals and falling leaves of autumn. The Buddha himself had his great Realisation on seeing the brilliance of the morning star. In the same way the mountains and rivers and sun and moon and stars, every morning and night, are preaching the sermon to bring us to realisation.

We should understand that it is never effective merely to rebuke others harshly. Let each of us keep to his own role and play it properly; then a beauty will manifest spontaneously; high and low will be affected and their conduct will change to harmony and virtue.

Since the self is a creation of the mind and good and bad too are from the mind (or, rather, correspond to the spiritual beauty or ugliness of the man), the first thing is to train the mind. Training produces a charm and power which appear externally and affect others. There are various ways and means in spiritual training, but the first thing is faith. One's faith may be true or false, right or mistaken, shallow or deep, high or low and so on, and Zen master Dogen warns us: 'Do not be led astray to the worship of godlings of the hills or other such, but believe in the teaching of the Buddha and prostrate yourself before the Buddha, the sublime incarnation of limitless power and virtue.'

When this reverent faith bubbles up in us, our everyday sinful nature of itself begins to shine with the light of compassion, and the beauty and power of the true Heart break forth and we move in harmony with the Buddha-light. When this happens the virtues of the Buddha-body are ever in our breast, from head to foot our action is prompted by the Buddha. Such is the life of faith, and in it every incident preaches the sermon of action.

Those who have not light in their hearts are always in darkness, a darkness in which a hundred demons come and go. Under their sway, life goes from darkness to darkness, ordinances of heaven are broken, the way of man is transgressed, and finally one is broken, to suffer the agonies of Hell.

Faith is all-important to man, and it is given to us by religion. There are different religions also, but in Japan Buddhism has come down in an unbroken stream for well over a thousand years and has deeply penetrated the life of the people. If today the people live in the faith of Buddhism and in the Bodhisattva spirit preach the sermon of action, we not only glorify our own people but demonstrate the sermon of no words to the peoples of the world, and this is the supreme task today.

2. STILLNESS IN ACTION

Stillness in the midst of action is the fundamental principle of Zazen (sitting in meditation). Some people think of Zazen as a sort of monopoly of the Zen sect, but the sect certainly has no monopoly of it. Zazen is the basis of the universe. Heaven and earth sit in meditation, every object sits in meditation. Knowing nothing of the Zen sect, all things are performing their meditation.

What is called Zazen means to live at peace in the true basis of the universe, which is stillness. Movement is a secondary attribution: stillness is the real condition. Out of stillness comes all activity.

For instance, the water of the ocean, when disturbance of wind ceases, at once goes back to the state of calm; the grass and trees, when the cause of agitation dies away, become as it were calm. These things always return to rest in the stillness which is their true nature. And this is the principle of Zazen. In nature there are day and night; when the sun sets gradually there is a hush, until what is called the dead of night when all is still as if a current of water had ceased to flow. This is Zazen of nature.

As with everything else, so with man. Working by day, we sleep at night. Falling into deep sleep, men forget the existence of self and are absolutely at rest. This is a state of what is called in Zazen 'body and mind loosed and dropped away'. In nature the counterpart of the restless action of day is the absolute stillness of night, and to abide in that is the principle of Zazen. In this sense everything naturally practises Zazen.

I may know nothing of Zazen, yet if I know what it is to sleep in bodily and mental relaxation then all unconsciously the benefits of Zazen rain upon me.

The Zazen of the Zen sect is to seek this way of stillness in the midst of activity. The method is to bring to stillness the mental activities, based on illusion, and conform to the stillness which is the fundamental nature of the mind.

When it is attained in Zazen, the result is called Satori or realisation. Zazen is practice of infinity, conforming to the infinity which is the principle of the universe.

Part Five

From a Commentary on Rinzai-Roku

by Omori Sogen, A Modern Japanese Zen Master

TRANSLATOR'S NOTE: Omori Sogen is a well-known Zen Roshi, who was formerly a master of Kendo, Japanese fencing. He is also an expert calligrapher. This commentary is on the recorded sayings and doings of the Chinese Zen Master Rinzai, who taught in the middle of the ninth century A.D.

Chinese words and names are rendered as the Japanese pronounce them. The old Zen master's name is rendered in modern Chinese Lin-chi, but this is no nearer to how he himself would have pronounced it than the Japanese approximation Rinzai.

In this translation I have omitted some Chinese places and names, and some references to Japanese works, which mean nothing to a modern Western reader.

It is a peculiarity of Zen style, ancient and modern, that they deliberately juxtapose classical phrases with colloquialisms and even slang; the reader has to be prepared for this.

RINZAI TEXT

The Governor and his officers invited the master to take the high seat. Going up the hall, the master said: 'If the mountain priest goes up on to this today, it is because there is no alternative; it is out of respect for the people. The tradition of our line of patriarchs and pupils is to hold the tongue. But then you would have nowhere to put a foot. In face of the governor's insistence, how can the mountain priest this day hide the great transmission?

'Well, is there here any skilful general to plant his banner and deploy his troops on the field? Let him bear his witness before everyone, and we will see!'

... Going up the hall meant mounting the dais in the main hall, either at fixed times or as occasion offered, to preach the doctrine for the monks. Today in the big temples of Japan the hall of the doctrine is kept for special ceremonies, and there is another hall for preaching. But in an ordinary temple the two are combined.

One day the governor of the country where Rinzai lived asked the master to give a sermon for him and a number of his officers. Rinzai ascended the seat and began by saying that though he has had to go up at the insistent request of the governor, really there is nothing to teach about Zen. But neither is it something which does not teach. It is beyond ordinary consciousness and its discriminations. Rinzai calls himself 'mountain priest', by which he means a man of the mountains ignorant of the world. It is a self-depreciatory phrase which he often uses.

Now he finds that to meet the wishes of the people, he has got to preach. From the Zen standpoint, the peak of Zen is neither this nor that. Zen expresses itself right before us – the sky high above and the earth below, the willow green, the flower red. With these things right in front of us, he says, *I* don't want to make a lot of hair-splitting distinctions. And you – you do not have to put a foot anywhere.

RINZAI TEXT

A monk asked what is the great meaning of Buddhism. The master gave a Katzu! shout. The monk bowed. The master said: 'That's a man who can hold his own in debate.'

COMMENTARY

As he spoke, a monk sprang forward. 'What is the great meaning of Buddhism?' What is the peak of Zen, he is asking. To put such a beginner's question, there in front of the governor and the officers and the ranks of Rinzai's disciples, shows no ordinary man. And almost before the words are out of his mouth, without an instant's gap, Rinzai shouts 'Ka!'

This shout, which is traditionally pronounced in Japan Ka(tzu),* is written with a Chinese character now pronounced in China Ho! and there have been those who believed that the shout should therefore be not Ka! but Ho! However, the sound does not have any meaning of itself. Or if it has to have one, then the Katzu! is to arouse to life directly an experience beyond all thinking and distinguishing and reasoning and feeling.

The monk was equal to the occasion, and to the Katzu! merely replied innocently, 'Thank you for the teaching', by carefully making a formal bow.

Rinzai said in appreciation, 'That's one who can hold his own!' – he is quite an opponent.

(*TRANSLATOR'S NOTE: It is thought today that this is another case where the Japanese pronunciation has kept closer to the original than the modern Chinese Mandarin, and that the shout was something like Ka!

The '-tzu' on the end of this transliteration from the Japanese is in fact not pronounced – it is a conventional way of showing that the sound is cut off short instead of dying away. It is a sort of glottal stop in the throat.

As a matter of fact English people pronounce a final 't' in much the same way in their ordinary conversation; so when they say 'I got the bread-knife but it wouldn't cut', the final 'cut' is similar to 'katzu' in Japanese. The 't' is not pronounced. A foreigner who does not know any English at all cannot make out what consonant the word is supposed to end with.

A shout similar to the Zen one is used in some of the Budo arts like Judo and Kendo, and also (piano) in music. It is given by abruptly tensing the abdominal muscles.)

RINZAI TEXT

The next one asked: 'And from whom is it, the song that you sing? To whom does your tradition go back?'

The master said: 'When I was with Obaku, I questioned three times, three times I was beaten.'

The monk hesitated. The master gave a Katzu! then hit him, saying: 'You can't fix a nail in space!'

COMMENTARY

The monk who came out next used a musical metaphor, 'From whom is it, the song that you sing?' No one training under Rinzai could fail to know that his tradition came from Obaku, so to ask about this well-known fact shows that he is no beginner. The master made a matter-of-fact reply, that when he was training under Obaku, he had three times asked what Zen is, and three times had been ruthlessly beaten. In this commonplace reply there is lurking a deadly poison.

The monk had perhaps been expecting that the master would give his usual Katzu! shout, and when instead there was this absolutely direct reply, he involuntarily 'hesitated'. This word means using one's judgment, reckoning where one stands, working out what one is going to say – all that sort of thing.

Suddenly Rinzai took him off balance with the favourite Katzu! and finished him off with resounding thwacks of his bamboo stick. So he went back.

'You can't drive a nail into space' – don't do your practice like a man hitting a nail into a bag of rice, was Rinzai's comment.

RINZAI TEXT

There was a master of the chair who asked: 'Are not the Three Vehicles and the Twelve Teachings enough to bring to light our Buddha nature?'

The master said: 'Your weeds are not yet hoed.'

The monk retorted: 'Why, how should the Buddha have beguiled people?'

The master said, 'Where is he, the Buddha?'
The preacher kept quiet.

'So', said the master, 'in front of the governor you would want to take me in, me the old monk! Go back at once, you are in the way of others.'

COMMENTARY

Next appeared a monk of one of the other sects. In the Buddhism outside the Zen sect, the main thing was preaching and study of the texts. As they were lecturers specialising in the theory of Buddhism, holding as it were what we should call a university chair in the subject, they were called masters of the chair, meaning masters of Buddhism.

This master of the chair came out and asked, 'Are not the Three Vehicles and the Twelve Teachings enough to bring to light our Buddha nature?' The three vehicles are those of the Shravikas, who hearing the Buddhist doctrine practise it for long months and years to become Arhats, of the Pratyeka-buddhas who attain enlightenment for themselves by cognition of the chain of causes of natural phenomena, and the Bodhisattva path which aims at enlightenment both for oneself and for others. These were said to be the three paths, and each man was by his nature and talents drawn to one of them. The twelve teachings were the so-called twelve divisions of the holy scriptures, and the phrase means roughly the whole body of scripture.

The master of the chair is urging that realisation of the true self is not limited to Zen, but that all who practise

Buddhism, and the texts themselves, are all aiming at this same thing.

To this Rinzai answered: 'Your weeds are not yet hoed.' What they call our Buddha nature, or our true self, is something absolute, and distinctions of words and explanations can never suffice for it.

'But then are the scriptures to be false? It cannot be so, the Buddha would never have deceived people.' The master of the chair did not understand what Rinzai meant, and did not realise that Rinzai was bringing him to realisation of the true self.

The Zen master says, 'The Buddha, after all where is he? Show him, here and now!"

Alas, the master of the chair does not seem to know that living Buddha, and he can only keep quiet.

'So you were wanting to take me in, before the governor, were you? Go back at once, you are in the way of the others.' Then the master of the chair having gone back, Rinzai goes on speaking:

RINZAI TEXT

And he added: 'It is for the One Great Matter that we are holding this meeting. Are there any more questioners? Let them come forward quickly and ask. And yet, even as you open your mouth, you are already off the point. How so? Don't you know that Buddha said:

The Dharma is other than words,
Neither limited nor conditioned?

Because your faith falls short, you get entangled. It is to be feared that the governor too and his officers will get tangled up and their Buddha-nature obscured. Better to retire!'

He then gave a Katzu! and said, 'You of little faith, one will never finish with you! I have kept you standing a long time – take care of yourselves.'

COMMENTARY

(He continued) 'Today's Dharma-meeting was for the One Great Matter, to know the real self. If there are any who have doubts about it, come out without hesitation. But if you fall into logic-chopping even a little, then it has nothing whatever to do with the real self As holy Buddha taught, the Dharma, the highest truth, has nothing to do with texts or words, or with causes and effects and so on, but it is the self eternally unchanging. So it is not something which is to be caught hold of. If you could catch hold of it, then that would not be the truth, the Dharma. This is where your faith wavers, because your thought, your belief, in the self has not been made firm. So now today's prating is over. Very likely the governor and his people are caught up in the tangle too. The more one talks about it, the more mud gets over the True Face, the Buddha-nature. Well, let me stop now.'

Rinzai said this and gave a Katzu! shout.

'O you of little faith, you'll never get it, even in a blue moon. I've kept you standing a long time – take care of yourselves,'and with these words he left abruptly.

RINZAI TEXT

One day the master went to the provincial capital, and the governor invited him to take the high seat. Then Mayoku came forward and asked: 'Kannon of Great Compassion has a thousand hands and a thousand eyes. Which eye is the true one?

The master said: 'Kannon of Great Compassion has a thousand hands and a thousand eyes. Which eye is the true one? Say it quick, quick!' Mayoku pulled the master from his seat and took it himself. The master went up to him and said: 'How goes it?' Mayoku hesitated. The master in turn pulled him down from the seat and resumed his place. On that Mayoku went out and the master came down.

COMMENTARY

One day something took the master to the provincial capital and there he called on the governor, who took the opportunity to ask Rinzai to preach. As it happened Zen master Mayoku was there, and he came out and asked: 'Kannon of Great Compassion with the thousand hands and eyes – which is the true eye?' This form of Kannon has a thousand arms and a thousand eyes and the question is which of those thousand eyes is the true one. But from the point of view of a Zen question-and-answer, it cannot be merely a child's riddle like that. It will be, 'The living Kannon, the true self, where is it?'

Rinzai immediately fires the question back, 'Where is the living Kannon, now speak, speak!' This is an action where the whole body has altogether become Kannon.

Mayoku without a word pulls Rinzai down from the high seat, and settles himself there in his stead – 'Look, make your bow deeply', he seems to be saying.

Now Rinzai comes up in front of him and says, 'How goes it?' This means something like Good-day or How Do You Do?

At this fresh response Mayoku hesitated. An ancient remarks that this hesitation is really an appreciation of Rinzai's move.

And now it is Rinzai who pulls Mayoku down from the chair and plants himself there.

Mayoku is silent and abruptly sweeps out. 'Nothing to ask' – and the ancient praises this exit as showing neither shadow nor substance.

Seeing it, Rinzai too comes down abruptly from the high seat – 'Nothing to answer'.

Would this be the living action of the Kannon of Great Compassion with the thousand eyes? Mayoku becomes Rinzai directly; Rinzai, just as he is, is Mayoku. There is the all-pervading humanity where self and others are one, and is this also the very body of the thousand-armed Kannon?

Daito Kokushi remarks on this piece of living theatre, 'After the rain, the breeze in the bamboos is cool', and indeed there is a breath of coolness about it like you get after the rain.

RINZAI TEXT

'On the lump of red flesh there is a True Man without Title, always coming out and in from your face. You who have not realised Him, look, look!' Then a monk came out and asked,

'What is this True Man without Title?' The teacher came down from the Zen chair and caught hold of him, 'Speak, speak!' The monk was at a loss. The teacher released him; 'True Man without a Title – oh, what is this dried shit-stick!' And he returned to his quarters.

COMMENTARY

This sermon in the Rinzai monastery itself, expressing Rinzai's fundamental Zen thought, has always been a much discussed one. The 'lump of red flesh' is sometimes taken as the physical heart, the organ itself, but it is better to take it as our five-foot-tall body. The True Man without Title should be taken as the real human nature, the true humanity which transcends all limitations or superimpositions such as the Fifty-two States of the Way, or differences of sex or social class, or the distinction of worldly and holy. One could call it the essential life.

This which is called the True Man without Title is said to be always from morning till night going out and coming in to our face. The word originally meant mouth but if we consider it in other contexts as used by Rinzai, it may seem proper to take it as the organs including the five senses, and even more widely to take in the hands and feet. But in this connection we must be careful that it is not something separate which exists within our physical body.

The centre of the development of Rinzai's thinking is this 'Man' – it pivots on that one word. Rinzai certainly does not mean a Buddha nature which is only a potential, nor a body nature which exists within; but his special standpoint is that this five-foot bag of shit itself is to be grasped as the True Man without Title.

Mu-I (without title) is sometimes expressed as Mu-E (without clothing) meaning transcendence of all dependence – absolutely naked without a stitch on. Since the Mu-I is the Mu-E, that man limited by his five-foot-tall body and his fifty years of life is the absolutely existent without any dependence. The True Man without Title, casting away the red lump of flesh itself, stands clear; the man of the way is an individual and at the same time transcends individuality – transcendent and at the same time individual.

In our physical body there is absolutely free human nature unlimited by anything at all. From morning to night, with the eye seeing things, with the ear hearing things, with the nose smelling odours, with the body feeling warm and cold, with the intellect appreciating things, with the hands grasping, with the feet walking – ever at work. Those who have not clearly realised this in experience, now, here, see and grasp it! So Rinzai said. Then a monk came out, 'What is this True Man without Title?' Rinzai jumped up from the chair where he was sitting, and quickly grasped the clothes at the other's breast: 'Speak, speak!' and glared at him fiercely. He sought to make the True Man without Title come into full operation. But the monk did not realise this, and hesitated, overwhelmed by the teacher's pressure. Rinzai let him go – dropping his hold abruptly – 'True Man without Title – what is this dried shit-stick!' This True Man without Title, what a useless idiot this is!

Then he went back at once to his own quarters.

List of Illustrations

1   Boat and sail, frontispiece 4
2   Monk carrying the load 12
3   Rinzai Zen monks engaged in walking meditation 101
4   Waiting for admission 102
5   The stick when bad posture indicates
    mind-wandering 103
6   Monk in meditation 134
7   Three sages laughing 166
8   Cleaning: work is done with enthusiasm 169
9   Dance of the Sennin 169
10 Actor with masks 184